MW01221733

CIVIL WAR

The War Between the States

BY
GEORGE LEE AND ROGER GASTON

COPYRIGHT © 1994 Mark Twain Media, Inc.

Printing No. CD-1828

ISBN 1–58037–007–1

Mark Twain Media, Inc., Publishers
Distributed by Carson-Dellosa Publishing Company, Inc.

Permission for the use of pictures from *The Dictionary of American Portraits* and *Gardner's Sketch Book of the Civil War* was obtained from Dover Publications, Inc., New York.

INTRODUCTION

The Civil War was the major dividing point separating America's youth from its adulthood. The heroes of this epic event are still larger than life: Lincoln, Lee, Jackson, and Grant. Each year thousands of Americans go to Civil War battlefields, debate the war in Civil War Roundtables, perform reenactments, and write and buy books and magazines concerning this four-year period in our history. It was a very complicated war, and young people need to understand what happened and why. This book is not for the adult who has a sophisticated knowledge of the war; it is for the young person who needs to learn the basic story as accurately as possible.

This book is intended to do more than tell about battles. We have also included information about how the struggle began, what Congress was doing, how the war affected the blacks, and information about army organization and the weapons of the war. Coverage of all events is far from complete, but the bibliography should point the potential Civil War buff toward books and articles that will help him or her do more reading on the topic.

Encourage your students to immerse themselves in the time period. Have them look at the "Challenges" questions not as a history review, but as "current affairs." Allow students to spend some time with the encyclopedia looking up those people who are most fascinating to them. Have them discuss the war in present tense with their family and friends. The cannons of Gettysburg are still roaring, Jackson is still on the loose in the Shenandoah Valley, Lincoln is still trying to find a general who knows how to win, and Robert E. Lee has become the most admired (or feared) military man since George Washington. Remind students that many young men, some 12 and 13, are in uniform as drummers. Their sisters are working with the women in preparing bandages and worrying about their fathers, brothers, and uncles who are facing death or injury on the battlefield this very day.

Decisions are being made and debated each day. Involve the class in those debates. "Points to Consider" may be used either for class discussion or writing opinions.

"The Bragging Contest" and the Union and Confederate leaders crossword puzzles can be used to reinforce student learning concerning the people involved in making the decisions of the Civil War.

"Whose Army Is This?" is an activity designed to illustrate the organization of an army and can be used with the chapter "Organizing the Two Armies."

In chapters dealing with specific battles, the names of southern military leaders are printed in italics. This is done to assist students in identifying which army the military leaders represent without constantly noting their affiliation within the text.

For many students, the Civil War is one of the most exciting periods in American history. Use that enthusiasm to foster interest in other historical studies. What students learn about the past may help them make better decisions in the future.

—THE AUTHORS

CIVIL WAR TIME LINE

Pre-Civil War era

1619	Africans brought to Virginia.
1780-86	Gradual freeing of slaves in northern states.
1787	Northwest Ordinance bars slavery in Northwest Territories.
1793	Fugitive Slave Law passed by Congress.
1800	Gabriel Prosser revolt in Virginia.
1816	American Colonization Society formed.
1820	Missouri Compromise.
1831	Nat Turner's Revolt.
1833	American Anti-Slavery Society formed.
1840	Liberty Party formed.
1846	Mexican War begins. Wilmot Proviso.
1850	Compromise of 1850.
1852	*Uncle Tom's Cabin* by Harriet Beecher Stowe published.
1854	Kansas-Nebraska Act. Republican party formed.
1857	*Dred Scott* decision.
1858	Lincoln-Douglas debates in Illinois.
1859	John Brown's raid on Harpers Ferry.
1860	Lincoln elected president.

Civil War (dates included for battles and major events)

December 20,1860	South Carolina secedes.

1861

1861	Mississippi, Florida, Alabama, Georgia, Louisiana, and Texas secede.
1861	Confederate States of America formed. Jefferson Davis elected provisional **president**.
March 4	Lincoln delivers inaugural address.
April 12	Firing begins on Ft. Sumter.
April 15	Lincoln calls for 75,000 volunteers.
1861	Virginia, Arkansas, Tennessee, and North Carolina secede.
1861	Western counties of Virginia organize Union government.
July 21	First Battle of Bull Run in Virginia.
August 10	Battle of Wilson's Creek in Missouri.
October 21	Battle of Ball's Bluff.
November 9	*Trent* affair angers England.

1862

1862	Edwin Stanton named Secretary of War replacing Simon Cameron.
January 19-20	Battle of Mill Springs in Kentucky.
February 6	Ft. Henry, Tennessee, captured by Grant.
February12-16	Ft. Donelson, Tennessee, captured by Grant.
March 7-8	Battle of Pea Ridge in Arkansas.
March 9	*Merrimac-Monitor* fight to a draw off Hampton Roads.
April 6-7	Battle of Shiloh in Tennessee.
April 7	Island No. 10 in Mississippi River falls to Federals after siege began March 16.
1862	CSA approves a draft of men from ages 18-35.
April 26	New Orleans occupied by Union troops under Butler.
May 4	McClellan occupies Yorktown, Virginia.
May 14	McClellan within 20 miles of Richmond; stops for reinforcements.
May 20	Passing of Homestead Act.
May 31-June 1	Battle of Fair Oaks Station east of Richmond; Joe Johnston wounded, and Robert E. Lee appointed to replace him.
June 26-July 2	Seven Days Battle in Virginia.
July 1	Pacific Railway Act charters transcontinental railroad.
July 2	Morrill Act grants land to states to create agricultural and mechanical colleges.

Civil War Time Line (continued)

August 29-30   Second Bull Run battle in Virginia.
September 17   Battle of Antietam, Maryland.
September 22   Lincoln issues Preliminary Emancipation Proclamation.
December 13   Battle of Fredericksburg in Virginia.

1863

January 1   Emancipation Proclamation.
March 1   Conscription Act drafts men between ages 20–45 for the Union army.
April 16-17   Union fleet passes guns at Vicksburg, Mississippi.
May 2-4   Battle of Chancellorsville in Virginia.
May 22   Siege of Vicksburg begins.
June 20   West Virginia admitted to Union.
July 1-4   Battle of Gettysburg.
July 4   Vicksburg surrendered to Grant.
July 13-16   New York draft riots.
September 19-20   Battle of Chickamauga in Tennessee.
November 19   Gettysburg Address.
November 23-25   Battle of Chattanooga (Lookout Mountain, Missionary Ridge) in Tennessee.

1864

May 5-6   Battle of the Wilderness in Virginia.
May 7   *Sherman's march through Georgia begins (Sherman's activities italicized).*
May 8-12   Battle of Spotsylvania in Virginia.
May 13-16   *Battle of Resaca in Georgia.*
May 25-28   *Battle of New Hope Church in Georgia.*
June 1-3   Battle of Cold Harbor in Virginia.
June 7   Republican National Convention picks Lincoln and Johnson as presidential and vice presidential candidates.
June 15-18   Petersburg withstands Grant's attack; siege of Petersburg begins.
June 19   *U.S.S. Kearsage* sinks *C.S.S. Alabama.*
June 27   *Battle of Kennesaw Mountain in Georgia.*
July 2-13   Jubal Early raids Maryland, comes within 5 miles of Washington on July 11.
July 30   Battle of Crater takes place at Petersburg, Virginia.
August 29   Democratic National Convention picks McClellan and Pendleton as presidential and vice presidential candidates.
September 2   *Federal troops enter Atlanta.*
October 31   Nevada admitted to Union.
November 8   Lincoln wins presidential election.
November 14   *Sherman's March to the Sea begins.*
December 15-16   Battle of Nashville in Tennessee.
December 22   *Sherman takes Savannah, Georgia.*

1865

January 15   Battle of Ft. Fisher, North Carolina.
February 17   *Columbia, South Carolina, burned.*
February 18   *Charleston, South Carolina, falls to the Union.*
March 4   Lincoln's Second Inaugural.
March 25   Battle of Ft. Stedman, Virginia.
April 1   Battle of Five Forks, Virginia.
April 2   Lee moves out of Petersburg.
April 3   Confederates surrender Richmond.
April 9   Lee surrenders at Appomattox Courthouse, Virginia.
April 14   Lincoln shot by John Wilkes Booth; dies April 15.
April 26   Booth killed near Bowling Green, Virginia.
April 26   *Joe Johnston surrenders to Sherman near Durham Station, North Carolina.*
May 10   Jefferson Davis captured.
May 26   Kirby Smith surrenders to Canby at New Orleans.

TABLE OF CONTENTS

Table of Contents (continued)

THE UNANSWERED QUESTION: THE MEANING OF UNION

Daniel Webster

The writers of the Constitution had done many things well, and for that wisdom they deserved the tribute of their nation. But a serious question had not been answered. Was this a union formed by the PEOPLE of the United States, or by the people of the United STATES? To us, this seems a trivial question, but it was one debated endlessly in the early days of the republic. James Madison, in opposing the Sedition Act in 1799, said that states had the right to *nullify* (cancel) unauthorized actions by Congress. New Englanders favored this position at the Hartford Convention during the War of 1812, and John C. Calhoun of South Carolina later developed that theory into a doctrine accepted by most southerners. Simply, the doctrine stated if Congress went too far, a state had the right to prevent a law from being enforced inside its boundaries.

Daniel Webster, during a debate with Robert Hayne, said in 1830 that if there is a problem with either the Constitution or the way it is being applied, the solution is to *amend* it. The Union had been good for the country, in every way, he said, and as long as it existed, the future was bright. He closed with the famous words: "Liberty *and* Union, now and forever, one and inseparable!" But by 1860 more than words were needed to settle the debate.

The United States were held together by a fragile cord by the 1850s. The differences were not just in what people said, but in the way they thought. The South preferred tradition; the North was excited by change. The South valued land, while the North found prosperity in business and trade. The South used slave labor, while the North used low-paid immigrants to do the hardest jobs in factories. The South gave power to aristocrats called planters; the North was governed by middle-class politicians.

The first time slavery became a big issue was in 1820 as Congress debated whether it should admit Missouri as a slave state. The deal was fashioned by Henry Clay, allowing Missourians to keep slavery if they chose. Those territories of the Louisiana Purchase south of 36°30' would be open to slavery; those north of that line closed to slavery. During debate, a few northern Congressmen called slavery a "sin," and their tone alarmed Thomas Jefferson like a "fire-bell in the night." The "Missouri Compromise" was accepted, and attention turned to less heated topics.

A solution to slavery that was popular at the time was colonizing—send the blacks back to Africa, or find an isolated place for them in Central America. Many leaders liked this idea, and the government bought a piece of African coastline that they named Liberia. However, northern blacks were opposed to colonizing; they considered themselves American.

Others, called abolitionists, opposed both colonizing and slavery. Their most well-known spokesman, William Lloyd Garrison, began his newspaper, *The Liberator,* in 1831. From then on, the fire-bell rang often.

Name _____

Class _____

POINTS TO CONSIDER

1. What difference did it make whether the "people" or the "states" had formed the United States?

_____

_____

_____

_____

2. If nullification were in effect today, how would it affect laws passed by Congress?

_____

_____

_____

_____

3. Do you think William Lloyd Garrison was popular? Why or why not?

_____

_____

_____

_____

Name _____

Class _____

CHALLENGES

1. What does "nullify" mean?

_____

_____

2. Who became known as the defender of nullification?

_____

3. Who used the phrase: "Liberty and Union, now and forever"?

_____

4. Which section of the country was most interested in farming?

_____

5. Which section of the country was more interested in business?

_____

6. What were southern aristocrats called?

_____

7. Who put the Missouri Compromise together?

_____

8. Where did it draw the line between territories open and closed to slavery?

_____

9. Why did Jefferson refer to the debate as "a fire-bell in the night"?

_____

_____

10. What was an abolitionist? _____

_____

THE SOUTH: OLD TIMES WERE NOT FORGOTTEN

The Lacy House in Falmouth, Virginia, was a symbol of the prosperity that many pre-war southerners hoped to attain.

If you look at a map of the United States in 1860, you may notice that the area of slave states looks larger than that of the free states. The South covered 896,000 square miles, and the North (excluding distant Oregon and California) only 557,000 square miles. Between 1820 and 1860, the South's population grew, but not as rapidly as the North's. This fact bothered the South because northern states would get larger majorities in the House of Representatives. After Nat Turner's slave rebellion in 1831, and with fear growing that abolitionists would stir up more trouble in the future, southerners saw trouble ahead.

Southern whites were not all alike. Extending all the way from Maryland and Delaware to Texas, the South's geography was a mixture of mountains and fertile valleys, forests and plains. The crops varied from one region to the next. Tobacco was the main crop of Maryland, Kentucky, and Virginia; hemp and corn in Missouri; sugar in Louisiana; and rice in the South Carolina lowlands. However, the crop that most represented the South was cotton.

In economic status and influence, there were great differences. At the top of southern society were the planters, owners of more than 20 slaves. The 1860 census included only 46,274 planters; less than 3,000 owned 100 or more slaves; only 11 held 500 or more slaves. The size of a plantation was limited by the time it took for a slave to reach the most distant fields, so a planter might own several plantations. In numbers they were few, but in economic and political influence the planters were powerful. Some lived in great mansions, but most preferred reinvesting their wealth in more land, horses, and slaves.

The merchant and professional class also had influence. Many of them also owned slaves, and some dreamed of the day when they would become planters. The largest customer of the merchant or lawyer and the largest contributor to the church was the planter, so attorney, merchant, and minister were all tied to the slave system. Owners of fewer than 20 slaves often had more invested in slaves than in horses and mules, so they also had good reason to keep the system going.

At the bottom of white society was "po' white trash"—people usually very thin, with yellowish skin, bad teeth, and addicted to cheap liquor and chewing tobacco. They were illiterate and isolated. However, their pride would not permit them to do the work of slaves. While not all poor whites fit this stereotype, they were definitely a class of people looked down upon by others. Richer people did not ridicule them (the men could vote); they just ignored them.

What did southern whites have in common? They had pride. They fought duels if someone insulted them, so they usually were well armed. Chivalry was part of life—the protection of the honor of white women and kin was a man's duty. Tradition was important; keep things the way they are, and don't allow changes that alter them. No Yankee was going to take the honor and property from a southerner without a fight.

Name _____

Class _____

POINTS TO CONSIDER

1. Do you think southerners all thought alike on most subjects? Why or why not?

_____

_____

_____

_____

_____

2. Why did planters have so much influence in the South?

_____

_____

_____

_____

_____

3. How do you think the common qualities of southerners helped make them defiant of the North?

_____

_____

_____

_____

_____

Name_____

Class_____

CHALLENGES

1. How large were the 15 slave states (in square miles)?

_____

2. What was the main crop of Maryland and Virginia?

_____

3. What were the main crops of Missouri?

_____

4. What crop was grown in Louisiana?

_____

5. What crop was regarded most highly in the South?

_____

6. What were the wealthiest southerners called?

_____

7. How many southerners owned 20 or more slaves?

_____

8. How many southerners owned 500 or more slaves?

_____

9. How were lawyers and ministers attached to slavery?

_____

10. How did pride keep the poor whites in poverty?

_____

_____

THE NORTH BEFORE THE WAR: EXPANDING FRONTIERS

Steamboats were rapidly being replaced by locomotives in the pre-war North.

As one crossed the Mason-Dixon line between Pennsylvania and Maryland, or traveled down the Ohio River on a steamboat, he found himself between two different worlds. The difference came from technology, transportation and communications networks, and attitudes.

Technology means to apply science and engineering to practical needs. Agriculture had benefited greatly from John Deere's steel plow (1837), Cyrus McCormick's reaper (1831), and other inventions like threshing machines and corn planters. These improvements caused farmers to head west to states like Illinois, Indiana, and Michigan. For each person in Indiana in 1830, there were four by 1860. During the same period in Illinois, the population increased 11 times, while Michigan's population was multiplied by 24. As farm production increased, it became possible to feed more people living in American cities and to export to Europe.

Agriculture in New England could not compete with that in the West, but the Northeast's economy was saved by progress in the textile industry. In the mills of Lowell, Massachusetts, and other cities, cloth was produced from southern cotton and northern wool. Inventions created new opportunities for investment and employment: sewing machines, elevators, pneumatic tires, revolvers, and typesetting machines among them.

Cities grew rapidly in the North and were centers of both production and commerce. By 1860, over a million people lived in New York, 565,000 in Philadelphia, 212,000 in Baltimore, and over 160,000 in both Cincinnati and St. Louis. City streets were clogged with wagons, carriages, and pedestrians. Poor immigrants fresh off the ship found rooms in city slums, where gangs and disease made their lives difficult.

Transportation and communication had been affected by new technology. To the dismay of those who owned turnpikes, stagecoaches, freight wagons, and steamboats, the railroads were coming on strong and taking their customers. In 1850, three northern states (New York, Pennsylvania, and Massachusetts) had over 1,000 miles of track. By 1860, five northern states had over 2,000 miles. Compared to the South, the North was far ahead; not only did it have more miles of track, but northern railroads were better equipped and maintained. The telegraph had been invented by Samuel F.B. Morse in 1841, and by 1860 there were 50,000 miles of line. The Trans-Atlantic cable was completed in 1858, but it broke a few months later.

Attitudes were different in the North. People were more religious and inclined toward reform movements; temperance, women's suffrage, and anti-slavery causes often drew the same individuals. Financial success was as important to them as counting slaves and landholdings were to southerners. Most northerners saw change as something desirable, and even those who did not felt that it was inevitable. To them, southern preoccupation with slavery seemed hopelessly out of touch with reality.

Name _____

Class _____

POINTS TO CONSIDER

1. In what ways was the northern farmer different from the southern farmer?

_____

_____

_____

_____

2. What difference do you think technology makes in fighting a war?

_____

_____

_____

_____

3. The South felt that its farmers made better soldiers than the northern shop owners and factory workers did. Would you agree or disagree?

_____

_____

_____

_____

Name _____

Class _____

CHALLENGES

1. How many times did Indiana grow between 1830 and 1860?

_____

2. Faced with western competition, what happened to New England agriculture?

_____

3. What inventions helped agriculture expand?

_____

4. What invention made taller buildings more acceptable?

_____

5. Name the three largest American cities in 1860.

_____

6. How many northern states had over 2,000 miles of railroad track in 1860?

_____

7. In what ways besides miles of track were northern railroads superior to southern railroads? _____

_____

8. Who invented the telegraph?

_____

9. How many miles of line had been strung by 1860?

_____

10. How did northerners feel about change?

_____

_____

CONTROVERSIES: WILMOT TO "BLEEDING KANSAS"

Harriet Beecher Stowe

It was not William Lloyd Garrison's *The Liberator* or southern nullifiers who created the Civil War. Most Americans were too busy working to worry much about these issues. By the 1840s, travel was mostly east-west, not north-south, so few in Georgia had ever met a New Yorker, and few Vermonters had ever met a Mississippian. Most northerners didn't care much about slaves and had no desire to either free them or have more blacks moving to the North.

It was frontier expansion that caused Congress and the people to wrestle with the slavery question. It had been important in the question of whether to bring Texas into the Union and became more of an issue when the Mexican War began in 1846. At that time, Representative David Wilmot of Pennsylvania offered a proviso (condition) that slavery not be permitted in any territory taken from Mexico. It passed in the House, but the Senate beat it back after southerners warned it might lead to secession (leaving the U.S.). However, the issue did not die and came up frequently in Congress.

The war ended as a great success in 1848; the U.S. gained 529,000 square miles of territory. During the next year, thousands of Americans crossed the continent to find gold in California; by 1850, it had a population nearing 100,000, and it wanted statehood. If accepted, there would be more free than slave states. The South would lose close Senate votes. Everyone realized how important the issue was, and some wanted to solve it.

The aging Henry Clay (a Whig) teamed up with ambitious young Stephen A. Douglas (a Democrat) to piece together what became known as the Compromise of 1850. It included: California to be admitted as a free state, New Mexico and Utah Territories organized with no reference to slavery, a stronger fugitive slave law, an end to the slave trade in the District of Columbia, and Texas would receive $10 million in return for giving up some land to New Mexico. Debate was hot. Northerners like William Seward (New York) and Salmon Chase (Ohio) attacked it, but so did Jefferson Davis (Mississippi) and John C. Calhoun (South Carolina). Daniel Webster spoke in favor of the compromise on March 7 and won over some Congressmen who were wavering on their vote. The Compromise was accepted; for a time, people felt better about the future of the U.S.

Publication of Harriet Beecher Stowe's novel *Uncle Tom's Cabin* in 1852 brought new converts to the abolition cause and made others wonder about how far they should go to cater to the South. Years later, Lincoln greeted Mrs. Stowe as "the little woman who made this big war."

"Bleeding Kansas" also contributed to the war. In 1854, Senator Douglas proposed the Kansas-Nebraska bill, creating two new territories, each with the option to allow slavery if the people chose. Many northerners protested this violation of the Missouri Compromise, which barred slavery from that region. The issue split Democrats, destroyed the Whigs, and created the Republican party. The resulting tension led to an assault on Charles Sumner on the Senate floor and murders and raids in Kansas.

Name _____

Class _____

POINTS TO CONSIDER

1. Why do you think the South was so furious over the Wilmot Proviso?

_____

_____

_____

_____

_____

2. What did North and South each get out of the Compromise of 1850? If leaders on both sides were angry, what does that say about the Compromise?

_____

_____

_____

_____

_____

3. In what way did the Kansas-Nebraska bill violate the Missouri Compromise agreement between North and South?

_____

_____

_____

_____

_____

Name _____

Class _____

CHALLENGES

1. Were most northerners enthused about ending slavery? _____

2. Who proposed that slavery be excluded in territory taken from Mexico?

_____

3. How did southerners manage to kill his proviso?

_____

4. How much land did Mexico lose after the Mexican War?

_____

5. What caused so many people to move to California?

_____

6. What two men were most important in getting the Compromise of 1850 through Congress? _____

7. Who were two southern critics of the compromise?

_____

8. Who was "the little woman" credited with starting the war? _____

9. Who proposed the Kansas-Nebraska bill? _____

10. A) What did its passage do to the Whigs and Democrats? B) What new party came into existence because of it?

Whigs? _____

Democrats? _____

New party created? _____

DRED SCOTT TO JOHN BROWN
1857-1859

John Brown

In 1856, the nation elected its 15th president, James Buchanan. A man who had a hard time making decisions, his position was made more difficult by the four southerners he picked for his cabinet and by the Supreme Court. In 1857, three days after Buchanan took office, the Court handed down one of its most controversial decisions. The Dred Scott case concerned a slave whose master, now dead, had taken him into territory declared free by the Missouri Compromise. Scott and his supporters felt this made him a free man, but the Missouri Supreme Court said it did not, and the case was appealed to the U.S. Supreme Court. Chief Justice Roger Taney handed down the majority decision. He said that Scott was not a citizen of Missouri or the United States, and the Missouri Compromise had been unconstitutional because territories existed "for the common use and equal benefit of all." The white South rejoiced that the Court agreed with them, but the ruling angered many northerners. It hurt the image of the Court at a time when its influence was needed to protect civil rights.

The Dred Scott issue spilled over into the election of 1858. Stephen Douglas's six-year term was up that year, and since at that time state legislatures still elected senators, he needed a Democratic majority in the Illinois legislature so he could be reelected to the Senate. His Republican opponent was Abraham Lincoln, a Springfield attorney. Of the two, Douglas was by far the better known. Lincoln, a Whig turned Republican, appeared to be outclassed by the eloquent, well-dressed Douglas, but Douglas was not fooled. Lincoln had an appeal to the backwoodsmen of Illinois with his tall, rugged appearance and his clever sayings. The two held a series of debates, the most famous of which occurred at Freeport, Illinois. Lincoln asked Douglas if the people in a territory could exclude slavery. Douglas said they could keep it out by passing unfriendly laws. Democrats kept control of the legislature and returned Douglas to the Senate. However, the debates made Lincoln famous and gave him a basis on which to run for president.

John Brown returned to the nation's attention in 1859. A failure in most ways, he had often been forced to flee from bad debts. A strong abolitionist, Brown was angered because others talked but did nothing. He had gone to Kansas and, during the turmoil there, raided a pro-slave community, brutally killing five men and boys. After a short stay in New England, he went to Missouri and stole 11 slaves and took them to Canada. He then planned an attack to free all slaves. After capturing the federal arsenal at Harpers Ferry, Virginia, he would arm the slaves of the area and begin a great revolt.

After capturing the arsenal, Brown's plan collapsed, and he was surrounded by militia and a company of marines led by army Colonel Robert E. Lee. Ten of Brown's men, including two of his sons, were killed when he refused to surrender. He was tried by the state, found guilty, and hanged. Some in the North said he was a hero, but others, including Lincoln, feared he had gone too far.

Name _____

Class _____

POINTS TO CONSIDER

1. As an abolitionist, why would the Dred Scott decision upset you?

_____

_____

_____

_____

_____

2. Who do you think gained the most from the debates: Lincoln or Douglas? Why?

_____

_____

_____

_____

_____

3. Do you feel John Brown was a person to be admired? Why or why not?

_____

_____

_____

_____

_____

Name _____

Class _____

CHALLENGES

1. How many days passed after Buchanan took office before the Supreme Court handed down the Dred Scott decision?

_____

2. According to Taney, was Dred Scott a citizen of Missouri or the U.S.?

_____

3. Why did he say that the Missouri Compromise was unconstitutional?

_____

_____

4. Who was Douglas's Republican opponent in 1858?

_____

5. Which Lincoln-Douglas debate was most famous?

_____

6. In that debate, how did Douglas say people could keep slavery out of a territory?

_____

7. Was it Lincoln or Douglas who went to the Senate?

_____

8. What had Brown done before that made him well known?

_____

9. Why did he choose to attack Harpers Ferry?

_____

10. How did Lincoln feel about the raid?

_____

THE 1860 ELECTION AND THE SECESSION CRISIS

By 1860, the aftermath of John Brown's raid was felt across the nation. Buchanan's image was hurt by scandals in his administration, and the Supreme Court was discredited because of the Dred Scott decision. Congress was hardly able to do business; anything one section proposed was opposed by members from the other section. Chaos was taking over.

Courtesy New-York Historical Society
Abraham Lincoln

All of this made the election of 1860 especially important. The Democrats met in Charleston, South Carolina, in April, and even though Stephen Douglas was popular with northern delegates, he lacked southern support. The convention adjourned without choosing a candidate and was to meet in June at Baltimore. Whigs and Know-Nothings joined forces that year and relabeled themselves as the Constitutional Union party. They chose John Bell (Tennessee) and Edward Everett (Massachusetts) as their candidates.

The Republican convention met in Chicago at a large wooden building called the "Wigwam." Two men had the largest delegate support: Lincoln and William Seward. The platform was written first, and it included the right of states to control domestic institutions (whether to have slavery), a railroad to the Pacific, a homestead act, and a protective tariff. The contest for president was hard fought, but Lincoln won the nomination on the third ballot. The vice presidential choice was Hannibal Hamlin of Maine.

When Democrats met again at Baltimore, they were no closer to agreement than they had been in Charleston. Southern delegates walked out; the northern delegates then chose Douglas as their presidential candidate. Southerners met again and chose John C. Breckinridge of Kentucky as their candidate.

There were no TV commercials or presidential debates in 1860 and very few speeches by the candidates. Southerners warned they would leave the Union if Lincoln was elected. That threat had been used before, and few Republicans believed the southerners were serious. Douglas, however, did believe them and campaigned in the South warning against the folly of secession.

Lincoln won a clear majority in the electoral vote with 180, Breckinridge 72, Bell 39, and Douglas 12. Lincoln won in northern states, Douglas and Bell in border states, and Breckinridge in the South.

Receiving promises of support from Mississippi and Alabama, South Carolina seceded December 20, 1860. In South Carolina, people cheered and bands played as the U.S. flag was taken down. Other states of the Deep South felt the same joy as they departed in January 1861. The Union was falling apart, and Buchanan was still president until March.

Buchanan did not know what to do. He opposed secession, but felt he had no right to force states to remain. Many Cabinet members, military people, and government employees supported the South, so no one could be trusted. By March 1861, seven states had left the Union and seized all federal property within their borders. Now only two spots remained in Federal hands: Ft. Sumter in Charleston's harbor and Ft. Pickens at Pensacola, Florida.

Name _____

Class _____

POINTS TO CONSIDER

1. The southern states warned that if Lincoln was elected, they would leave the Union. Why did that not cause more northerners to vote for Douglas?

_____

_____

_____

_____

2. Bell and Douglas both did best in the border states (slave states along the line between free and slave states). Do you think there was any reason for that?

_____

_____

_____

_____

3. President Buchanan seemed unable to solve the secession crisis. List problems he faced in holding the Union together.

_____

_____

_____

_____

Name _____

Class _____

CHALLENGES

1. Who was the favorite candidate in 1860 among northern Democrats?

_____

2. What kept him from getting the nomination at Charleston?

_____

3. What groups joined to form the Constitutional Union party?

_____

4. Whom did the Constitutional Union party choose for president?

_____

5. Whom did northern Democrats run for president in 1860?

_____

6. Who ran for president on the southern Democratic ticket?

_____

7. Which candidate did the most campaigning?

_____

8. How many electoral votes did Lincoln get?

_____

9. What were some problems Buchanan had in dealing with southern secession?

_____

_____

10. By the time Lincoln came into office, what two forts in the South still remained in Federal hands?

_____

SUMTER FORCES DECISIONS IN THE UPPER SOUTH

Courtesy New-York Historical Society
Robert Anderson

As Lincoln made the journey from Illinois to Washington, D.C., he gave no indication as to how he planned to handle the situation at Ft. Sumter, where Major Robert Anderson and his men were within range of South Carolina cannons in Charleston Harbor and were running out of food and supplies. In his inaugural address, Lincoln said it was up to the South to decide if there would be war; at the end, he said: "I am loath to close. We are not enemies but friends. We must not be enemies." This appeal was directed mostly to the loyal citizens of the border slave states who were watching and deciding which way they should go if fighting began at Ft. Sumter.

Lincoln moved very slowly at first, waiting for Unionist sentiment to develop in states like Virginia, Maryland, Kentucky, and Missouri. His lack of action caused even Cabinet members to wonder if he was up to the job. The South was also waiting, hopeful that he would surrender Ft. Sumter without a fight and let the South leave the Union without a war.

Patience was wearing thin on both sides, and the new Confederate president, Jefferson Davis, feared that South Carolina would soon act on its own unless he pressured Anderson to leave Ft. Sumter. He sent orders to General *P.G.T. Beauregard* to demand surrender. *Beauregard* sent officers to the fort, and Anderson told them he would run out of supplies April 15 unless he was reprovisioned. *Beauregard* seized the opportunity and told Anderson firing would begin on the fort in one hour. At 4:30 a.m., on April 12, 1861, shelling began and continued for 30 long hours. Anderson surrendered the fort on April 14, and he and his men were allowed to leave by ship.

The next day, Lincoln called on governors to supply 75,000 militia who would serve 90-day enlistments. Governors of border states now faced the moment of truth. Would they commit their men to a war against their friends in the South and support a Federal government that, in the view of many, threatened states' rights and the institution of slavery?

Southern unionists were in an uphill battle to influence their states' decisions, and even they felt that the Federal government must guarantee states' rights. When Lincoln did not give them the answers they wanted, Virginia, Arkansas, Tennessee, and North Carolina left the Union. Governor John Ellis of North Carolina wrote Lincoln: "I can be no party to this wicked violation of the laws of the country and to this war upon the liberties of a free people." The Confederacy had grown from seven to eleven states.

Many in the other four slave states (Delaware, Maryland, Kentucky, and Missouri) also wanted to secede, but Lincoln was determined to use any means to keep them from leaving the Union. Governor Beriah Magoffin of Kentucky declared his state neutral and refused to send state militia to aid either side. Maryland's governor was loyal, but many in the legislature were not, and 19 were arrested. Governor Claiborne Jackson of Missouri wanted secession, but Unionists were strong enough in the state to prevent him from succeeding.

Name _____

Class _____

POINTS TO CONSIDER

1. What risk would the South have taken if they had waited until April 15 to attack Ft. Sumter?

_____

_____

_____

_____

_____

2. Do you think it was a good idea for Lincoln to put border state governors on the spot by requesting militia? Argue for or against.

_____

_____

_____

_____

3. Do you think Lincoln's handling of the Maryland legislature was right or wrong? Argue for or against.

_____

_____

_____

_____

Name _____

Class _____

CHALLENGES

1. Who was commander at Ft. Sumter?

_____

2. Who was the Confederate commander at Charleston?

_____

3. Whom was Lincoln trying to convince with his inaugural address?

_____

4. When did the shelling of Ft. Sumter begin?

_____

5. How many militia did Lincoln request from governors?

_____

6. What did his request of militia for 90 days suggest to you?

_____

_____

7. How did Governor Ellis of North Carolina react? _____

_____

8. How did Governor Magoffin of Kentucky react? _____

_____

9. How did Lincoln handle the Maryland legislature? _____

_____

10. Which side did Governor Jackson of Missouri favor?

_____

WAR LEADERS COMPARED: LINCOLN vs. DAVIS

National Archives, Brady Collection

Abraham Lincoln (left) President of the United States of America
Jefferson Davis (right) President of the Confederate States of America

Jefferson Davis was disappointed when he was chosen president of the Confederate States of America (CSA). Unlike Lincoln, who had worked hard to become U.S. president, Davis did not want the job; he would have much preferred being a general. His wife, Varina, wrote that his main talent was military: "He did not know the arts of the politician and would not practice them if understood."

In experience, Davis had an impressive record. Educated at Transylvania University and West Point, he had been an army officer in the Northwest and was wounded in battle during the Mexican War. His legislative career included terms in both the House and Senate. In 1853, he became Secretary of War. He returned to the Senate in 1857, where he remained until 1861. He opposed secession, but after the decision was made, he supported it.

Lincoln's record was shorter. Born in Kentucky, his family had migrated to Illinois. He never attended college, but he read enough to qualify as a lawyer. His military service was a brief stint as a militia captain during the Black Hawk War in 1832. He wrote that he never even saw an Indian and never bent a sword in battle, but he had many bloody encounters with mosquitoes and bent his musket once by accident. He served one term in the state legislature and one term in Congress.

In some ways the two men faced similar situations. Both came under fire from the press and were accused of acting like dictators. Each had a Congress that seemed more concerned about getting friends into high places and offering unhelpful suggestions than winning the war. Each wasted valuable time at long cabinet meetings instead of letting the heads of departments do their jobs. Each showed personal courage in dangerous situations. Lincoln walked through the streets of Washington accompanied by only one bodyguard, even though there were many rumors of plots against his life. Davis tried to stop bread rioters in Richmond by himself. Both men carried the burden of long casualty lists and many citizens accusing them of not doing everything possible to end the conflict.

The main difference between the two was that Lincoln was far superior as a politician. Often exhausted and tense, he listened carefully to those who lined up outside his office "for a brief word." He visited military hospitals shaking hands with the troops, knowing that their relatives voted. Lincoln often delayed making decisions until public opinion was strongly behind the policy he intended to pursue in the first place. Davis did not play the political game, stubbornly pushing unpopular policies.

Perhaps the greatest compliment paid to Lincoln during his lifetime was by the southern newspaper, the Charleston *Mercury,* which said that he ran the presidency with "a bold, steady hand, a vigilant, active eye, a sleepless energy, a fanatic spirit . . . with an energy as untiring as an Indian, and a singleness of purpose that might almost be called patriotic."

Name _____

Class _____

POINTS TO CONSIDER

1. If an election were held today, and the two candidates for president were Lincoln and Davis, which would you support and why?

_____

_____

_____

_____

_____

2. Do you think military experience makes a president a better commander in chief of the army and navy? Why?

_____

_____

_____

_____

_____

3. In 1832, Lincoln wrote that he had "no other [ambition] so great as that of being truly esteemed* of my fellow men, by rendering myself worthy of their esteem." What was he saying, and do you think he succeeded in that ambition?

*Esteem means to be regarded with respect and admiration.

_____

_____

_____

_____

_____

Name _____

Class _____

CHALLENGES

1. Where was Jefferson Davis educated?

_____

2. In what war had he served?

_____

3. What jobs had he had in government besides his career as a soldier?

_____

4. What was Lincoln's profession?

_____

5. In what war had Lincoln served?

_____

6. What job had he had in the Federal government?

_____

7. How did Lincoln show courage?

_____

8. How did Davis show courage?

_____

9. Why did Lincoln sometimes move slowly before making a policy?

_____

_____

10. How did Lincoln show a concern for public opinion?

_____

ENTHUSIASM FOR WAR RUNS HIGH IN NORTH AND SOUTH

Winfield Scott

Few Americans could remember the last large war on American soil. It had been nearly 50 years before and had produced heroes like Andrew Jackson, William H. Harrison, and Oliver Perry. Even fewer were alive who could remember the American Revolution, with its heroes like George Washington, Lafayette, Lighthorse Harry Lee, and Nathaniel Greene. The most recent war had been fought in Mexico (1846-48), with Zachary Taylor and Winfield Scott leading armies to victory at places with names like Monterrey, Buena Vista, and Cerro Gordo. A veteran of that war might have told youngsters about the good old days and battles won against armies twice their size.

No one expected this war to last long. Lincoln's call for 90-day service in the army indicated his belief that the war would be short. Southerners talked about "Battle Summer" and believed that by fall, victory would be certain. Past wars had all been small. Only 4,435 had been killed in the American Revolution, 2,260 in the War of 1812, and 1,733 in the Mexican War. Americans had read about wars in Europe, like the Napoleonic Wars, and the more recent Crimean War (1854-56), where lives had been wasted by disease and hopeless charges like that of the Light Brigade. With no TV news reports to give eyewitness accounts of the war, the American public, both North and South, went into the Civil War in a good mood and a burst of patriotism. The only fear was that those cowardly Yanks (or Rebs) would surrender before the man could enlist in his nation's service.

This was a young man's war, and both armies were composed mostly of men between 17 and 21 years old. Even some officers were very young. The youngest brevet (temporary) major general was 17-year-old Galusha Pennypacker (USA). William P. Roberts (CSA) was 20 years old, the youngest Confederate brigadier general. Winfield Scott, ranking general of the U.S. Army, was 75 when the war began. Robert E. Lee (CSA) and Joseph Johnston (CSA) were both 54. In their 40s were generals William T. Sherman (USA), P.G.T. Beauregard (CSA), Jubal Early (CSA), George Meade (USA), and Joseph Hooker (USA). In their 30s were George Pickett (CSA), George McClellan (USA), Stonewall Jackson (CSA), and Ulysses Grant (USA).

There was a rush of men to sign up with militia companies, and ambitious politicians recruited new companies. Militia duty had always been almost a fun activity, and men were impressed by promises of beautiful uniforms and fine horses to ride in cavalry units. Mothers and wives busily made uniforms for husbands and sons. The most colorful units were the Zouaves, dressed in gaudy colors, with baggy pants, open jackets, and turbans or fezzes. There was no point in having a war without a fine uniform.

When orders came for the unit to move, the whole community turned out; bands played, flags flew, and there were tearful farewells, as the town saluted its brave young heroes marching off to war.

Name _____

Class _____

POINTS TO CONSIDER

1. What differences do you see in attitudes about war now than the mood in 1861?

_____

_____

_____

_____

_____

2. Why do you think it was more important then for officers to be young and in good health than it is today?

_____

_____

_____

_____

3. Do you think it was a good idea for units to be formed by communities, or should the soldiers have been mixed in with troops from other states? Explain.

_____

_____

_____

_____

_____

Name _____

Class _____

CHALLENGES

1. What indicated that southerners expected the war to be short?

_____

_____

2. In which American war before the Civil War had the most men been killed?

_____

3. In which American war before the Civil War had the least men been killed?

_____

4. What European war had been the most recently fought?

_____

5. What age group composed most of both armies?

_____

6. Who was the youngest brevet general in the war?

_____

7. Who was the youngest Confederate general in the war?

_____

8. Name three Union generals who were in their 40s.

_____

9. Name two Confederate generals who were in their 30s.

_____

10. If you saw a soldier wearing a fez, you would know he was in a _____ unit.

ORGANIZING THE TWO ARMIES

Inspection of Troops, Pamunkey, Virginia May 1862

In the weeks following secession, both the Union and Confederacy issued a call to arms and began a mad rush to organize their growing numbers of untried volunteers into effective armies. The net result was two American armies, both composed mainly of volunteer units. The two armies were similar in structure. The Union army had an established way of organizing its forces. Since many Confederate officers came out of that army, they organized the same way.

Both armies were organized into Territorial Departments (the area where they would be used) and then into smaller units. Confederate armies were named after the state or the region in which they operated. One Confederate army was the Army of Tennessee, for example. The Union armies were named after the major river flowing near where they operated. It had an Army of *the* Tennessee. Both sides then had smaller units that operated inside this larger "army."

The smallest unit was the **company.** Companies were hometown volunteer units, with most members coming from the same town or county. This would make the horror of war very real when the company suffered heavy losses in battle. In the Union army, companies had from 83 to 101 officers and men. Confederate companies were not so tightly controlled. Company officers included a captain, two lieutenants, five sergeants, eight corporals, and a teamster (wagon driver). Early in the war, the men elected company officers, but by 1862, both armies held examinations to choose officers. This weeded out incompetents and appointed better-qualified men to lead the units.

Regiments were composed of companies. Infantry regiments contained 10 companies, but cavalry regiments were composed of 12. In both armies, regiments were commanded by a colonel; other officers were a lieutenant colonel, major, adjutant (assistant to the commander), quartermaster, three surgeons, and a chaplain. As the war continued, new soldiers were not put into old regiments, but new ones were started. Regiments were numbered by the order in which they formed and their state; for example, the 3rd Vermont Cavalry, or 5th Virginia Infantry.

Brigades were composed of two or more regiments, with both armies assigning four or five regiments to a brigade. In the Union army, brigades were numbered (3rd Brigade), while Confederates named their brigades after their commanding officer (Hood's Brigade). In both armies, brigades were commanded by a brigadier general.

Divisions were made up of two or more brigades. Divisions were commanded by staff officers, major generals, or lieutenant generals.

Corps (pronounced "cores") were made up of at least two divisions, with three being the most common. They were given Roman numerals to identify them, such as III Corps. In the Union army, major generals commanded them; in the Confederate army, lieutenant generals were the commanders.

Name _____

Class _____

POINTS TO CONSIDER

1. If your company suffered heavy losses in battle, and you were one of the few to return home after the war, how would you feel? Why?

_____

_____

_____

_____

_____

2. If you were elected captain of your company and were ordered by the regiment to send your men into battle, how would you feel? Why?

_____

_____

_____

_____

3. Why was it important for the two armies to adopt competitive exams to choose officers? How would you feel if you were an elected officer of your company, failed the exam, and lost your rank?

_____

_____

_____

_____

Name _____

Class _____

CHALLENGES

1. What was meant by a "Territorial Department"?

_____

2. How were Territorial armies named in the Union army?

_____

3. How were Territorial armies named in the Confederate (CSA) army?

_____

4. Why were heavy casualties in a battle so important to small towns?

_____

_____

5. Early in the war, how were company officers selected?

_____

6. What rank did a regiment commander usually have?

_____

7. How many companies were in a cavalry regiment?

_____

8. How were brigades named in the Confederate army?

_____

9. How many brigades made up a division?

_____

10. How many divisions made up a corps?

_____

THE INSTRUMENTS OF WAR: INFANTRY, ARTILLERY, CAVALRY

Battery D, 2nd U.S. Artillery, Fredericksburg, 1863

By the time of the American Civil War, European armies had defined the roles of the three major branches of warfare. It remained only for the leaders of the two American armies to adapt these roles to their struggle. With minor differences, the Union and CSA used them in the same ways.

The **infantry** was the backbone of both armies. War, in the 19th century, was a "stand up and shoot it out" affair. Both armies maneuvered their troops into battle lines at ranges of 300 yards or less and swept the enemy line with thousands of large-caliber musket balls. Firing was normally "by the book," with officers ordering their men to "load-aim-fire" in separate commands. In this way, they controlled the timing as well as the volume of fire. This is referred to as "firing by volleys." Many soldiers were poor shots, and controlled firing by thousands of muskets at the same time had a way of making up for bad marksmanship.

Hours were spent drilling infantrymen according to the "Manual of Arms," teaching the soldier to handle his musket the same way every time he loaded and fired. After many drills, every man did the same thing at the same time. Much time was spent teaching soldiers to march and maneuver in unison. Moving large numbers of men into position in the heat of battle was as important as actually firing at the enemy. Once in position, the usual practice for the attacking army was to fire several volleys, then charge, using bayonets attached to the muzzles of the muskets. When a charge began, it was impossible for the defenders to get off more than one or two volleys, so everything depended on the courage of both armies.

The last moments of the charge were always the most critical, since it always ended in hand-to-hand combat. After the battle, bodies of dead and injured infantrymen littered the battlefield.

Artillery was vital to a battle. Civil War cannons had a fairly short range (1,500-2,500 yards for most), but they could reach the enemy at longer distances than muskets. If a defending general had enough cannons, he might break up a charge before it got close enough to succeed. Artillery fired a variety of shells: solid cannonballs, explosive shells (shrapnel), or canister (small iron balls). In a siege, artillery had a deadly effect, lobbing exploding shells into the enemy line, day and night if necessary.

The **cavalry** consisted of mounted soldiers that could do many things. They were lightly equipped and lightly armed, so they could move quickly. Weapons included a revolver and saber for mounted fighting and a short rifle (carbine) for fighting on foot. General Lee called the cavalry "the eyes of my army" and used it to scout Union positions. Cavalry also rode rapidly to support infantry, dismounting and filling gaps in the line when they arrived. Because cannons were so hard to turn, cavalry could charge at artillery positions from the side, kill the gun crews, and capture the guns.

Name _____

Class _____

POINTS TO CONSIDER

1. A well-trained infantryman took about 20 seconds to load a musket. If you were in battle, how would you feel as you charged into an enemy line, facing musket balls and bayonets?

_____

_____

_____

_____

2. If you were a general rating your army of infantry, cavalry, and artillery, what order would you put them in when it came to mobility (speed with which they can move), fire power, and importance in a battle? Why?

_____

_____

_____

_____

3. Of the three branches, in which do you think you would rather serve? Why?

_____

_____

_____

_____

Name _____

Class _____

CHALLENGES

1. What branch was called the "backbone of the army"?

_____

2. Teaching the soldiers to handle their muskets in the same way was done according to this book.

_____

3. What was the critical point in an infantry charge? Why?

_____

_____

4. What were two uses for artillery?

_____

_____

5. What was canister?

_____

6. What was the range of most Civil War cannons?

_____

7. As a cavalryman, what weapons would you have?

_____

8. Why did Lee call the cavalry the "eyes of my army"?

_____

_____

9. Why might a cavalryman be used on foot in battles?

_____

_____

10. Did cavalry charge directly in front of artillery positions?

_____

ARMS OF THE CIVIL WAR

Colt .44, New Model Army

(Detail, Colt .44) Rachet Loading Lever

Minie Balls

Colt Rifle Musket .58

Springfield .58

Sharps .52

Pistol and Shoulder Arms, USA

Wars always bring changes in technology as each army tries to find an advantage to use over the other. Such was the case in the Civil War. A demand for more, improved weapons inspired inventors to produce new designs. These included both small arms and artillery.

The Civil War was a rifleman's war. It was the infantryman with his rifled musket who determined the outcome of battles. Rifling was not a new idea. Gunmakers had long known how to machine spiral grooves in the bores of guns to make bullets spin in flight and be more accurate. During the Civil War, the muzzle-loading rifle was brought to the height of its development.

Rifled muskets of the time were accurate up to a half mile, and they were powerful. They fired bullets called minie [min-ee] balls, more than one-half inch in diameter and one inch long. They were made of soft lead and expanded on impact, making horrible wounds. The guns were muzzleloaders, loaded by ramming powder and bullet down the barrel with a ramrod. Breechloaders, some of them repeaters, were available in 1861, but were looked down on by old-fashioned officers who feared the easy loading would cause men to waste costly ammunition. Despite this, new designs were eventually used and accepted by the ordinance departments. President Lincoln personally tested two lever-action repeating rifles, the 16-shot Henry and the seven-shot Spencer, on the White House lawn and approved them. Repeaters were scarce, due to their higher cost and longer manufacturing time. More common were breechloading single shots like the Sharps, that could be fired three times as fast as a muzzleloading rifled musket. Breechloading carbines were popular among cavalrymen, who liked their rapid loading and light weight.

Sam Colt had produced his first revolver in 1836, but the Civil War saw new models that were lighter, more accurate, and more durable than older models. Revolvers were carried by officers, cavalrymen, and some artillerymen.

In 1861, the U.S. used a mixture of old, obsolete muskets, both American and foreign made. By 1862, manufacturing had caught up with demand, and no more foreign purchases were made. The South imported weapons throughout the war, made a few, and captured many from the North.

There were a variety of artillery pieces. Some had rifled cannon bores, others did not. Both sides prized the three-inch rifle (cannon), made of iron and firing a ten-pound shell. The "Napoleon," with its bronze barrel, fired a 12-pound shot and was also very popular. Huge cannons were used in forts and on ships. Bore sizes ran up to 12-15 inches, and they could fire 125-pound shells up to 5,000 yards.

The CSA developed underwater mines (called torpedoes) that floated just below the surface. They were designed to explode when struck by a ship. Mines sank 32 Union ships, seven of them ironclad.

The Civil War has been called "the first modern war" because of new developments in weapons and changes in tactics that made full use of the new arms available.

Name _____

Class _____

POINTS TO CONSIDER

1. As a soldier carrying a muzzleloader, how would you feel when you faced a soldier armed with a repeater?

_____

_____

_____

_____

_____

2. The North used newer types of weapons than the South. How would you explain why that happened?

_____

_____

_____

_____

_____

3. What were some new weapons of the Civil War that would be improved upon and used in later wars?

_____

_____

_____

_____

_____

Name _____

Class _____

CHALLENGES

1. Why does war advance technology?

_____

_____

2. Why was the Civil War a "rifleman's war"?

_____

_____

3. Why was a breechloader better than a muzzleloader?

_____

_____

4. Why did some army officers dislike breechloaders?

_____

_____

5. Who personally tested the Henry and Spencer repeating rifles?

_____

6. What Civil War soldiers might have been seen wearing holsters with revolvers in them?

_____

7. What were the two most popular artillery pieces?

_____

8. What was the range of 12- and 15-inch guns?

_____

9. How many Union ships were sunk by Confederate torpedoes?

_____

10. Why is the Civil War called the "first modern war"?

_____

_____

_____

BULL RUN: THE FIRST MAJOR TEST OF THE WAR

Ruins of Stone Bridge, Bull Run, Virginia

After Ft. Sumter fell, most Americans, North and South, believed the war would be short, with one major battle deciding the outcome. When the Confederacy chose Richmond, Virginia, as its capital, it seemed certain that the clash would occur somewhere in the 100 miles that separated the CSA capital from Washington. The Confederates established a defensive line along Bull Run Creek to shield an important railroad junction at Manassas, Virginia.

The new Union army of 39,000 men created by President Lincoln's call for 90-day volunteers was commanded by General Irvin McDowell. General Robert Patterson also had 11,000 men to threaten Harpers Ferry, Virginia. In June, General *P.G.T. Beauregard,* victor at Ft. Sumter, took command of the Bull Run line, while General *Joseph Johnston* guarded Harpers Ferry.

Time was running out for Lincoln's 90-day army, and Washington politicians were spoiling for a fight. McDowell pleaded for more time, but was ordered to move by late July. "On to Richmond!" was the slogan of the day. Patterson's troops captured Harpers Ferry in early July, and *Beauregard* braced for an attack. McDowell marched into Virginia on July 16, 1861. The weather was brutally hot, and his new soldiers were soft. McDowell rested his men at Fairfax Courthouse on the 17th. The 18th and 19th were spent at Centerville while he perfected his battle plan and chose the 21st as the day of attack.

While McDowell delayed, *Beauregard* gathered his forces and waited. On the 18th, *Johnston* was ordered to move his troops to Manassas Junction. When *Johnston* arrived with half of his troops, he took command of the CSA forces there. All of *Johnston's* field commanders were either West Point graduates or Mexican War veterans. McDowell's officers were not as well trained and experienced.

Instead of a mass attack, McDowell attempted a series of small frontal attacks. The southerners divided their duties, with *Beauregard* directing the defense and *Johnston* sending fresh troops where they were needed. The attack began early on the morning of the 21st, but McDowell's efforts were hampered by picnickers out to watch the glorious battle. His wagons had a hard time moving through the carriages of the sightseers.

At first it seemed McDowell's attack would succeed. Colonel David Hunter's 6,000 men crossed Bull Run Creek at Sudley Springs Ford and drove three CSA brigades back. The three retreating brigades climbed Henry House Hill, where they found General *Thomas Jackson* waiting patiently with a full brigade in battle formation. General *Bee* stopped the retreating troops, shouting: "There stands Jackson, like a stone wall." The three brigades joined *Jackson's* line. McDowell ordered two artillery batteries to soften up the southern line at Henry House Hill, but they were wiped out. At 3:30 p.m., two fresh CSA brigades attacked McDowell's right flank. *Beauregard* then ordered a general attack, and by 4 p.m., McDowell's army was in retreat. Chaos took over as carriages and cannons, soldiers and picnickers scrambled back to Washington; however, *Johnston* did not pursue because his men were too tired and disorganized to follow.

37 *Southern military leaders are in italics.

Name _____

Class _____

POINTS TO CONSIDER

1. If you were Beauregard, how would you feel as you waited for the Union attack?

_____

_____

_____

_____

_____

2. How do you think northerners felt about the war after the defeats at Ft. Sumter and Bull Run?

_____

_____

_____

_____

_____

3. If you were a soldier in McDowell's army after the battle, how would you feel when you saw the road ahead clogged with spectators?

_____

_____

_____

_____

Name _____

Class _____

CHALLENGES

1. Why did everyone expect the first battle to be fought between Washington and Richmond?

_____

_____

2. Why was Manassas important to the Confederates?

_____

_____

3. Why was the North in a hurry to fight a decisive battle?

_____

_____

4. Once he started, why was McDowell so slow to march against Bull Run?

_____

_____

5. How did Jackson get the nickname of "Stonewall"?

_____

_____

6. How did Johnston move his troops to Manassas?

_____

_____

7. What mistake did McDowell make in his attack?

_____

_____

8. What unusual problem did McDowell have in moving his troops to Bull Run?

_____

_____

9. What CSA move stopped the Union attack?

_____

_____

10. Why didn't Johnston attack the defenseless Union capital?

_____

THE CSA MAKES MAJOR DECISIONS

**The Stars and Bars,
First Official Flag of the Confederacy**

How do you start a government from scratch, knowing that war may be fast approaching? As leaders from southern states gathered in Montgomery, Alabama, in February 1861, there was little time for original thinking, and they hurriedly wrote a constitution similar to that of the U.S. Jefferson Davis was chosen as provisional president, and the vice presidency went to Alexander Stephens of Georgia. Stephens, instead of helping Davis, often worked against him and criticized Davis's policies.

In May 1861, the capital was moved to Richmond, a larger city with a more comfortable climate. Only about 100 miles from Washington, Richmond was also important because of its Tredegar Iron Works. The Union's struggle to capture Richmond and the South's determination to hold it made that decision important in the story of eastern campaigns.

The militia units making up the Confederate army were dressed in almost every style of uniform. The official color was cadet gray, but not enough dye was available to have all units dressed the same. Many soldiers dressed in butternut-colored uniforms (made by boiling nut shells and iron oxide filings). Most men dressed in whatever they came with or could afford. Even generals rarely dressed in fancy uniforms. The soap shortage made cleanliness an extravagance, and many were without winter coats, blankets, shoes, or boots. Like the Union army, cavalry wore yellow stripes on their pants, artillery wore red, and infantry wore blue.

The first official flag was the "Stars and Bars," (blue field in the left corner, a white stripe between two red stripes). At Bull Run, *Beauregard* saw flags of new troops arriving, but could not tell whether they carried U.S. or Confederate flags. That caused a battle flag to be adopted in September 1861. It had a red field with a large blue X, and it is the flag most commonly associated with the Confederacy. Meanwhile, the "Stars and Bars" was still being used, but its similarity to the "Stars and Stripes" caused confusion, so in 1863, the "Stainless Banner," with a battle flag in the upper left corner and a white field, was adopted. However, when there was no wind, it looked like a flag of truce, so the "Last National" flag was adopted in March 1865; it had a broad red bar across the end of the Stainless Banner.

Two other decisions affected the South's economy. One was to borrow money rather than tax the citizens. They were not used to paying taxes directly to Washington, and their loyalty at this point was seen as more important than their money. Instead of taxing, the CSA would borrow by selling bonds. Then they started printing money without any backing. When the South won battles at the war's beginning, people accepted the money, but after disasters in 1863, it became almost worthless.

Another important decision was to stop selling cotton to Europe. The idea was to cause mass unemployment at textile mills and force England and France to recognize Confederate independence. It did cause some unemployment in English textile mills, but its greatest effect was to hurt the South's ability to buy supplies and arms.

*Southern military leaders are in italics.

Name _____

Class _____

POINTS TO CONSIDER

1. Why might the choice of Richmond as Confederate capital have been a mistake?

_____

_____

_____

_____

2. The Confederate battle flag is often seen today. What do you think it means to those who use it?

_____

_____

_____

_____

3. Who do you think is hurt the most when runaway inflation (rapidly rising prices) occurs?

_____

_____

_____

_____

Name _____

Class _____

CHALLENGES

1. What constitution did the Confederate constitution resemble?

_____

2. Who was chosen as Confederate president?

_____

3. Who was the Confederate vice president?

_____

4. What city was chosen to replace Montgomery as capital?

_____

5. What was the official color of Confederate uniforms?

_____

6. How was fabric dyed a butternut color?

_____

_____

7. What was the first official Confederate flag called?

_____

8. Who suggested the need for a battle flag?

_____

9. What was the problem with the "Stainless Banner"?

_____

_____

10. What caused the value of Confederate money to drop rapidly?

_____

WELLES vs. MALLORY: BATTLE OF THE BLOCKADE

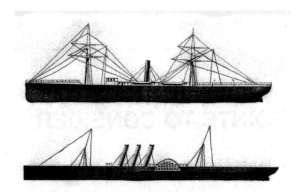

Ships of this type were used by blockade runners to smuggle goods in and out of the South.

Lincoln's choice for Secretary of the Navy was politician and newspaper editor Gideon Welles. Hard-working, focused on the task he faced, and totally loyal to Lincoln, he made an excellent Cabinet member. His chief assistant was Gustavus Fox, a former naval officer. Together, they took on many difficult assignments during the war. The navy gave support to military operations and was vital to the success of Grant, Butler, and others. The main task of the ocean navy was to keep cotton from leaving the South and arms and supplies from coming into southern ports.

Five days after Ft. Sumter fell, Lincoln ordered a blockade from South Carolina to Texas. After Virginia and North Carolina seceded, their coastline was included. The purpose was to keep the CSA from shipping its products to foreign ports and, more importantly, to keep arms and needed supplies from reaching the South. The job was easier said than done. The area covered totalled 3,550 miles. The U.S. navy had 90 ships (only 42 of which were in commission). Three ships were in the East Indies, and 23 were in the Pacific. Obviously, the blockade would be useless until the navy was greatly enlarged, and that was exactly what Welles set out to do. He recruited 20,000 sailors from merchant ships and purchased 100 boats of all varieties; the only requirement was they must be able to support guns. Another task was to capture harbors on the Confederate coastline that the blockaders could use for coal and supplies. Port Royal, between Charleston and Savannah, was captured and became a supply base for the blockaders.

At first, it was easy for ships to run the blockade, but in time it began to tighten and forced the South to find new ways to break it.

The CSA counterpart to Welles was Stephen Mallory, former senator from Florida and perhaps the most original thinker in the Cabinet. His task was to find ways to break the blockade with very little expense. He took the sunken steamer, *Merrimac,* and turned it into the ironclad *Virginia.* The CSA also tried building submarines. The first attempts were unsuccessful, and many crewmen's lives were lost. But eventually the *CSS Hunley* sank the *USS Housatonic* by use of a mine attached to a long pole. The explosion, however, also destroyed the *Hunley.*

Commerce raiders were sent out to attack northern shipping to force the Union navy to pull ships out of the blockade line to chase them. Some raiders were very successful. The *Alabama,* commanded by Raphael Semmes, captured or destroyed 64 vessels, including a Union gunboat. The *CSS Shenandoah* was the only Confederate ship to go around the world, and it captured 30 ships. In total, the raiders captured 200 ships, with damages of $15-20 million.

Fast, long, and sleek blockade runners were privately owned and carried needed supplies to the Confederacy. As the blockade tightened, many were captured. Welles had won the contest, but Mallory had proven himself a worthy competitor.

Name _____

Class _____

POINTS TO CONSIDER

1. What common characteristics did Welles and Mallory share?

_____

_____

_____

_____

_____

2. Which of them (Welles or Mallory) did the best job? Why did you choose him?

_____

_____

_____

_____

_____

3. Why do you think it is that people usually do not associate navies with the Civil War?

_____

_____

_____

_____

_____

Name _____

Class _____

CHALLENGES

1. How long was the Confederate coastline?

_____

2. If the 42 ships in the Union navy were evenly scattered along that coastline, how much territory would each have covered?

_____

3. What was the most important reason for having the blockade?

_____

_____

4. What was the first major supply base for the blockaders?

_____

5. Who was the CSA Secretary of the Navy?

_____

6. What was the original name of the *Virginia?*

_____

7. What was the first submarine used in battle?

_____

8. What was the first victim of a submarine attack?

_____

9. What commerce raider was commanded by Semmes?

_____

10. Which raider went around the world?

_____

FT. HENRY AND FT. DONELSON: GRANT'S RISING STAR

Ulysses S. Grant

Ulysses S. Grant, who had left the army in 1854, returned in 1861 with the help of political pull. No one could have guessed what a major part he was destined to play in the Civil War. His fame spread rapidly after his first two battles at Ft. Henry and Ft. Donelson. Three important water routes flowed north to south, cutting into the western part of the Confederacy: the Mississippi, Tennessee, and Cumberland Rivers. To discourage invasion, the CSA fortified "Island Number 10" on the Mississippi, Ft. Henry on the Tennessee, and Ft. Donelson on the Cumberland. These water routes were too tempting for the Union to ignore. In February 1862, Brigadier General Grant began planning to open the Tennessee and Cumberland Rivers to Union shipping.

Flag Officer Andrew Foote from the navy commanded the gunboats that supported Grant's attacks. Two full divisions of troops aboard steamboats were covered by seven gunboats. The troops were landed four miles from Ft. Henry, and on February 6, 1862, the gunboats attacked the fort. Heavy rains had raised the river's level, and Ft. Henry was partly flooded. The fort's commander, General *Lloyd Tilghman*, had sent most of his troops to Ft. Donelson, 12 miles away, keeping only a few artillerymen to defend the fort. Taking advantage of the high water, Foote's gunboats came so close to Ft. Henry that many of the fort's guns could not be turned on his boats. At point-blank range, he hammered the fort for two hours. Outgunned and undermanned, *Tilghman* surrendered. The Tennessee River was open to Union attack all the way into Alabama.

Ft. Donelson was not as easy. It lay on high ground and was well fortified. It had 21,000 defenders to take on Grant's 15,000 men, but Foote's gunboats evened up the odds. Foote attacked on February 14, but his guns did little damage to the fort. The fort's guns found their mark, sinking two gunboats and damaging the rest. Grant called off the attack and moved his troops in for a siege. The weather was very cold, and Grant's men burrowed into the fall leaves to keep warm. Grant needed help to succeed, and fortunately for him, it came from the CSA commanders at the fort.

Gideon Pillow attempted to break through Grant's lines and open a path to Nashville, Tennessee. Colonel *Nathan Bedford Forrest's* cavalry led the attack over the snow; by noon, he had cleared the way, but *Pillow* lost his nerve and returned. Inside the fort, tempers flared. *Forrest* was naturally furious with *Pillow* for retreating. *John Floyd* gave in to *Pillow* in the dispute, and *Floyd and Pillow* decided to surrender the fort. Since neither of them wanted that responsibility, they passed it on to *Simon Buckner,* the third man in charge. *Forrest* vowed he would never quit and took his 700 cavalrymen out before *Buckner* could meet with Grant.

When *Buckner* asked for the terms, Grant answered: "unconditional surrender." Newspapers became excited by that statement and printed glowing accounts of this new general who had brought home two major victories.

Name _____

Class _____

POINTS TO CONSIDER

1. The cooperation of army and navy in these two campaigns was unusual because the two had rarely cooperated before. What qualities do you think it took for Grant and Foote to work together as well as they did?

_____

_____

_____

_____

2. As a Forrest cavalryman, what would you be thinking when you learned that Ft. Donelson was about to be surrendered?

_____

_____

_____

_____

3. The northern press was high in its praise of Grant for these battles. Do you think he won because he was so good or because the CSA officers were so poor?

_____

_____

_____

_____

Name _____

Class _____

CHALLENGES

1. Why were the Cumberland and Tennessee Rivers important?

_____

_____

2. Who was in charge of Grant's gunboats?

_____

3. How did the gunboats take advantage of high water?

_____

4. How long did it take to capture Ft. Henry?

_____

5. Why were gunboats less successful against Ft. Donelson?

_____

6. Name the three CSA generals at Ft. Donelson.

_____

7. Who led the cavalry charge out of Ft. Donelson?

_____

8. Why did the breakout attempt fail?

_____

9. Who surrendered the fort to Grant?

_____

10. What terms did Grant give for the surrender?

_____

MERRIMAC vs. *MONITOR:* BATTLE OF THE IRONCLADS

***USS Monitor* (right) battles the *CSS Virginia (Merrimac)* (left).**

The CSA began the war without a navy, but its secretary of war, Stephen Mallory, began early to correct that problem by building ironclads.

When the Union abandoned its shipyard at Norfolk, Virginia, they burned and left behind a steamship called the *Merrimac.* Confederate engineers raised the hull, which had not burned below the waterline. Renamed the *Virginia,* the entire ship was covered with heavy iron plates, and it was armed with 10 heavy cannons capable of firing 100-pound shells. With its armor, guns, and powerful steam engines, it was more powerful than any Federal ship. News of its construction caused panic in Washington. Assistant Secretary of the Navy Gustavus Fox asked: "Who is to stop her from steaming up the Potomac and throwing her hundred-pound shells into the White House, or battering down the hall of Congress?"

"Who" turned out to be Swedish-born inventor John Ericsson. Secretary of the Navy Gideon Welles begged him to do something to stop the *Virginia.* Ericsson designed a strange looking ship resembling a cheesebox on a raft. The *Monitor* had a low, flat deck with a small rotating turret in the center that contained two guns. She was launched January 30, 1862, just 101 days after plans left the drawing board. The design was radical, and she was not very seaworthy. The *Monitor* was modified and finally sailed out of New York Harbor headed for the Virginia coastline.

On Saturday, March 8, 1862, laundry was being washed and hung to dry on the rigging of ships blockading the Virginia coastline. The *Virginia* chose this as the day to come out and fight. She plowed through the water toward the *USS Cumberland.* The *Cumberland's* captain described the *Virginia* as resembling a crocodile with an iron hide and guns and a long ram projecting forward. The *Cumberland* opened fire, but its cannon balls bounced off the *Virginia's* iron hull. The *Virginia* rammed the *Cumberland,* splintering her hull, then opened fire at point-blank range. The *Cumberland's* guns were still firing as she sank beneath the waves. The *Virginia* then destroyed the *Congress* and drove the *Minnesota* aground before withdrawing for the night. The crew decided the *Virginia* could finish off the *Minnesota* in the morning.

At 1 a.m. the next morning, the worried sailors on the deck of the *Minnesota* saw the *Monitor* pull alongside. Six hours later, the *Virginia* returned to destroy the *Minnesota,* but found a new opponent in her way. For four and one half hours, the ironclads battled in the shallow waters off Hampton Roads, Virginia. The ships were so close they collided five times, while the men loaded and fired as fast as they could. Finally, the *Virginia* withdrew after ruling the sea only one day. In their struggle, these two iron ships made every wooden naval ship in the world obsolete.

Neither ship fought again. The *Virginia* was blown up by the Confederates two months later to keep her from being captured. The *Monitor* sank in a storm off Cape Hatteras, North Carolina, in December 1862. After revolutionizing naval warfare, the two ships disappeared, but their memories linger on.

49

Name _____

Class _____

POINTS TO CONSIDER

1. As a sailor on the *Minnesota,* how would you feel when you saw the *Monitor* appear to save you from the *Merrimac?* Why?

_____

_____

_____

_____

_____

2. If you were an official in a foreign government, what questions would you ask about your navy after learning of this battle?

_____

_____

_____

_____

3. Old navy men were not impressed with the design of the *Monitor.* Write a report that they might have given on this new ship.

_____

_____

_____

_____

Name _____

Class _____

CHALLENGES

1. Which Confederate official believed ironclads were critical to victory?

_____

2. After salvaging the *Merrimac,* what name did the CSA give her?

_____

3. How was the former *Merrimac* changed in appearance, and how was she armed?

_____

_____

4. Who was the U.S. Secretary of the Navy?

_____

5. Who designed and supervised construction of the *Monitor?*

_____

6. What was the date that the *Monitor* was launched?

_____

7. What were Federal sailors doing the day the *Virginia* attacked?

_____

8. How many Union ships did the *Virginia* sink?

_____

9. Where did the ironclads fight their famous battle?

_____

10. Which of the ships was deliberately destroyed? _____

Which went down in a storm? _____

McCLELLAN'S PENINSULAR CAMPAIGN OF 1862

Battery No. 1, near Yorktown, Virginia
May 1862

Bull Run showed the North that a long war lay ahead of them. The aged General Winfield Scott was replaced by George McClellan as commander in chief of the North's army. He improved the men's spirits and organized the broken volunteer force into an effective army.

Washington and Richmond were separated by only 100 miles, and each side shaped its plans around capturing the other's capital. McClellan wanted to try reaching Richmond by attacking from the east rather than the north. He did not want to move until his army was much larger than that of the Confederates; the problem was that in his mind, the South's army was always much larger than it actually was. Lincoln finally ordered him to attack, and on March 17, 1862, McClellan moved 12 divisions by ship to Ft. Monroe on the tip of the peninsula formed by the James and York Rivers.

To prevent more Federal troops from joining McClellan, *Robert E. Lee* suggested that *Thomas Jackson* threaten the Federal armies in the Shenandoah Valley. Moving so quickly they became known as "Jackson's foot cavalry," *Jackson's* troops caught Federals by surprise one time after another. *Jackson* then rejoined the main CSA force facing McClellan.

Federal troops began moving toward Richmond on April 4, but found their way blocked the next day by earthworks thrown up by *John Magruder's* small army of 10,000 men. Even though McClellan had a larger army, he waited for more men to arrive and ordered a siege. That gave the Confederates time to move most soldiers in the region to oppose him. *Joe Johnston* was given command of the Yorktown line. McClellan prepared to attack that line, but by the time he was ready, *Johnston's* army had pulled back to stronger positions near Richmond. McClellan moved his base up to West Point, at the head of the York River. McClellan divided his army, with some north and others south of the Chickahominy River.

Johnston saw this as an opportunity and attacked the Federals south of the river at Fair Oaks. *Johnston* was seriously wounded, so command of the army was given to *Robert E. Lee. Lee* sent *Jeb Stuart* with 1,200 cavalrymen to discover enemy positions and strength. *Stuart* rode behind McClellan's army, gathered information, tore up a railroad, took prisoners, and with his mission completed, led his men back around the enemy. McClellan was so shocked by this that he moved all but the V Corps south of the river and built defenses at White Oak Swamp.

Lee took advantage of McClellan's caution. He called his generals together: *Jackson, Longstreet, and A.P. Hill.* He decided to send most of the army to crush the V Corps north of the river. Once it was destroyed, McClellan would have to retreat, ending the threat to Richmond. The risk in the plan was that by moving his troops north of the river, he could only leave 20,000 men south of it; they would be outnumbered by 70,000 Federal troops. Considering McClellan's reluctance to act, *Lee* took the risk.

Name _____

Class _____

POINTS TO CONSIDER

1. It is a mistake to believe an enemy is weaker than it really is. How did McClellan prove that it is also a mistake to believe the enemy is stronger than it really is?

_____

_____

_____

_____

_____

2. What do you think might have been important reasons for any general to be as successful as Jackson was in the Valley Campaign?

_____

_____

_____

_____

_____

3. If you were Robert E. Lee, what conclusions might you make about McClellan, and how might you use that insight to your advantage?

_____

_____

_____

_____

_____

Name _____

Class _____

CHALLENGES

1. Whom did McClellan replace as commander in chief of the Union army?

_____

2. How did McClellan want to reach Richmond?

_____

3. How many divisions did McClellan use in the Peninsular Campaign?

_____

4. Who was the first CSA general to block McClellan?

_____

5. Why was McClellan's decision to lay siege to Yorktown a mistake?

_____

_____

6. What divided McClellan's army after he set up headquarters at West Point?

_____

7. Why did Lee take command of the Army of Northern Virginia after the battle at Fair Oaks?

_____

8. Whom did Lee send to scout out Union positions?

_____

9. What fact about McClellan caused Lee to send most of his army to attack V Corps?

_____

_____

10. How many men faced the 20,000 men Lee left south of the Chickahominy River?

_____

THE SEVEN DAYS BATTLE

Led by *A.P. Hill,* CSA troops struck Fitz-John Porter's V Corps at Mechanicsville on June 26, 1862. *Hill* had once proposed to Ellen Marcey, who rejected him and married McClellan instead. When *Hill's* troops slammed into V Corps, a Union officer muttered: "For God's sake, Nelly, why didn't you marry him?" V Corps withdrew that night after a battle costing *Lee* 1,500 men. A series of battles known as the Seven Days had begun. *Lee* was determined to hold Richmond and force McClellan off the peninsula.

Military bridge across the Chickahominy River, Virginia. Fitz-John Porter burned a bridge of this type in order to escape the Rebel army.

On June 27, *Hill* struck Porter again. Porter had moved his men back to a small creek, and the battle took place at a grist mill called Gaines Mill. Porter was able to withstand that attack, but was then hit by *Longstreet,* assisted by *Jackson.* Porter asked for help, and McClellan sent him one division. McClellan still believed most of *Lee's* army was south of the Chickahominy River. Facing impossible odds, Porter crossed the river, then burned the bridge he had used. That night, McClellan began his retreat toward Harrison's Landing on the James River. The next day, while McClellan's army moved through White Oak Swamp, CSA engineers repaired the bridges, and the southern army started in pursuit.

The Federal retreat was covered by a strong rear guard defense. On the 29th, *Lee's* army attacked in and around a peach orchard near Savage's Station. The battle was halted when a severe thunderstorm struck at sundown. McClellan was so badly shaken that he ordered army supplies burned so the retreat could move faster. The next day, the two armies battled at Frayser's Farm. Then McClellan halted his forces and prepared to fight at Malvern Hill. McClellan ordered Porter to defend the hill with V Corps and any other troops he needed. He also gave Porter every cannon available.

Malvern Hill was on a 150-foot-high plateau with swamps to the east and west and the James River nearby. With the only good approach to the hill from the north, Porter concentrated his 250 cannons in that direction, and he also had gunboats in the river to add firepower.

The Confederate attack got off to a poor start and went downhill from there. The artillery was pounded by Federal cannons. As the Rebel infantry attacked, they were cut down by the artillery. *Major General D.H. Hill* said: "It was not war—it was murder." The South lost many more men in these battles than the Federals did, but McClellan had lost his courage, and instead of attacking, he backed off to Harrison's Landing on the river.

On July 6, Lincoln sailed down to see McClellan. The Union commander insisted he had not lost; he had failed to win because he was outnumbered. Estimates put McClellan's army at 150,000 and *Lee's* at 95,000. Lincoln ordered the army withdrawn to Washington.

Richmond had survived the threat. McClellan had shown that he could organize an army, but was a poor general in battle. *Lee* had shown that he was willing to take risks and could tailor his strategy to fit his opponent's personality.

Name _____

Class _____

POINTS TO CONSIDER

1. You have heard the expression: "Don't burn your bridges behind you." In Porter's case, was that a good idea?

_____

_____

_____

_____

2. How do you think Lincoln felt about McClellan's failure to take Richmond? Do you think that opinion was justified?

_____

_____

_____

_____

3. If you were McClellan, how would you feel when you learned that President Lincoln was coming down to talk with you?

_____

_____

_____

_____

Name _____

Class _____

CHALLENGES

1. Who led the attack on V Corps on June 26, 1862?

_____

2. What did Porter do to slow down the Confederates chasing him?

_____

3. What did McClellan do to make it easier to retreat?

_____

4. Why did McClellan choose to make a stand at Malvern Hill?

_____

_____

5. Who was ordered by McClellan to defend Malvern Hill?

_____

6. How many cannons did the Federals have on Malvern Hill?

_____

7. Who described the battle as "murder"?

_____

8. What reason did McClellan give Lincoln for failing?

_____

9. How many more men did McClellan have than Lee?

_____

10. What characteristics did Lee show in the Seven Days Battle?

_____

_____

THE CONFEDERATE HIGH COMMAND

Robert E. Lee

In the early days of the war, both North and South struggled to find generals who could lead armies into battle and win. By 1862, the CSA had found a group of officers able to produce victories, even without having all the supplies their opponents had.

Robert Edward Lee (1807-70) of Virginia, son of a Revolutionary War hero, graduated second in his West Point class and served in the Mexican War. In 1860, he was a colonel, U.S. 1st Cavalry, and was offered command of the Union army, but refused it when Virginia seceded. He resigned his commission to serve the South, and by war's end was commander in chief of the Confederate army. Lee proved to be a capable field commander who had an amazing ability to think on the move and outguess his opponent. One has to wonder how different the war would have been if he had taken command of the Union army.

Thomas J. (Stonewall) Jackson (1824-63) was a brilliant field commander who had also graduated from West Point and served in the Mexican War. When the Civil War began, he was a professor at Virginia Military Institute. He was appointed a colonel of Virginia Volunteers when the war broke out, but became a hero and a general after he earned his nickname of "Stonewall" at First Bull Run. He was also known as "Lee's right arm," because the two worked so well together. His best battle, Chancellorsville, was also his last. He was badly wounded and soon died after being shot by one of his own men who, in the darkness, mistook him for a Yankee.

James Longstreet (1821-1904) was also a West Point graduate and Mexican War veteran who chose to fight for the South. He proved to be a successful corps commander as long as he worked under Lee, but did not do nearly as well when he was on his own. He served faithfully and well, but was unpopular in the South after the war because of three things: (1) he argued with Lee over the wisdom of sending Pickett's men forward at Gettysburg, (2) he was right about the charge, and (3) he later became a Republican.

Jubal Early (1816-1894) was another West Point man and Mexican War veteran. He had a vengeful attitude that made him a terror in battle. He irritated Union troops so much that Grant ordered "veterans, militiamen, and everything that can be got to follow" and destroy him. Early reportedly said he liked pro-union towns "because they burn so nicely."

James Ewell Brown (Jeb) Stuart (1833-64) had graduated from West Point and fought in Indian wars. He was the best known Confederate cavalryman and literally rode circles around Union armies. He practically forced the Union to improve its cavalry by making them look so bad.

Joseph Johnston (1807-91) gave up a brigadier general's commission to serve the South. His arguments with President Davis kept him from being as successful as he might have been and caused him to be relieved of command at Atlanta. However, he was highly regarded as an opponent by Sherman.

 *Southern military leaders are in italics.

Name _____

Class _____

POINTS TO CONSIDER

1. After reading about Lee in an encyclopedia, why do you think he has always been so highly regarded by the South?

_____

_____

_____

_____

_____

2. Does a general always have to win to be considered great? Why or why not?

_____

_____

_____

_____

_____

3. Should President Davis have let his personal dislike for Johnston influence his decisions about him? Why or why not?

_____

_____

_____

_____

_____

Name _____

Class _____

CHALLENGES

1. What U.S. brigadier general resigned to join the Confederate army?

_____

2. Which general liked Unionist towns "because they burn so nicely"?

_____

3. In what branch did J.E.B. Stuart serve?

_____

4. How did Stuart make the Union army look bad?

_____

5. Where was Jackson teaching when the war began?

_____

6. Where was Jackson killed?

_____

7. What had Lee's father done that made him famous?

_____

8. If someone said Lee was cautious (very slow to act), would that be an accurate statement?

_____

9. Who was considered to be Lee's "right arm" in the early part of the war?

_____

10. What general especially disliked Early?

_____

THE BATTLE OF NEW ORLEANS

David Farragut

For the Union to be successful, it was necessary to take control of the Mississippi River and cut the Confederacy in two. In the spring of 1862, the U.S. navy began attacking southern strongholds on the river. In April, John Pope captured the CSA fortress at New Madrid, Missouri, called Island Number 10. On June 6, the Union fleet outgunned CSA gunboats at Memphis, Tennessee; now, two thirds of the river was in Union hands.

While those two victories were being won, a move designed to seize the rest of the river was taking shape. Flag Officer David Farragut was ordered to lead a fleet of 24 ships down the eastern seaboard and attack the port of New Orleans from the south.

Confederate officials had made Farragut's job very difficult. Forts Jackson and St. Philip stood opposite each other below New Orleans, both strongly built and well armed with heavy artillery. Between the two forts stretched a line of disabled ships, blocking the river to force attacking ships within easy range of the forts' guns.

Farragut's foster brother, Commander David Porter, proposed to solve the problem by sailing a small flotilla of ships, each armed with a 13-inch mortar, to a point just below the forts and shell them into rubble so the main fleet could pass safely. But after shelling Ft. Jackson for a week, the fort still remained strong. Farragut decided on a more daring move. Under the cover of darkness, he would steam past the forts, smash through the barricade, and attack New Orleans.

During the night of April 23–24, two gunboats came up river and cut loose several hulls blocking the channel. At 2 a.m., Farragut's fleet started past the forts, but the rising moon revealed the fleet, and the guns of the forts opened fire. The first Union vessel was hit 42 times. Farragut later said it felt like he was facing all the artillery on earth. His flagship, the *Hartford,* caught on fire, but the crew put out the flames. By dawn, nearly all of Farragut's ships were past the forts. At New Orleans, a makeshift squadron of eight ships came out to fight, but Farragut's guns sank six of them in minutes, the other two surrendered, and New Orleans fell without a shot being fired by the defending army.

The fall of New Orleans was a serious loss to the South, but the Mississippi River was not yet under Union control. Farragut continued upriver, taking Baton Rouge, Louisiana, and Natchez, Mississippi. But severing the CSA required taking the city of Vicksburg, Mississippi, located on a bluff 300 feet above the river, safely above Farragut's guns. It would require an army to take Vicksburg.

Farragut became a hero and America's first rear admiral. President Lincoln named Ben Butler military governor of New Orleans. He became very unpopular and was often referred to as "Beast Butler." He declared that slaves in the New Orleans area were free, and slaves flocked to the city from nearby plantations, further hurting the southern war effort.

Name _____

Class _____

POINTS TO CONSIDER

1. Looking at a Civil War map, why was capturing New Orleans and other Mississippi River cities so important?

_____

_____

_____

_____

_____

2. What could the South have done differently that might have prevented Farragut's success?

_____

_____

_____

_____

_____

3. If you were a loyal southern citizen of New Orleans, what would your reaction have been to the performance of the army defending your city?

_____

_____

_____

_____

_____

Name _____

Class _____

CHALLENGES

1. Why was it so important for the Union to get control of the Mississippi River?

_____

_____

2. Where was Island Number 10 located?

_____

3. What two forts protected New Orleans from attack?

_____

4. What had been done to force attacking ships to come nearer to the forts?

_____

_____

5. What gave away the presence of Farragut's fleet on the night of April 23-24?

_____

6. How much resistance did Farragut meet at New Orleans?

_____

7. What other Mississippi River cities did Farragut capture?

_____

8. Why was Farragut unable to capture Vicksburg?

_____

_____

9. How was Farragut rewarded for his achievements?

_____

10. Whom did Lincoln appoint as military governor at New Orleans?

_____

THE BORDER WAR

Early in the war as states chose sides, four states hung in the balance: Maryland, Delaware, Missouri, and Kentucky. All were slave states, but each had strong Unionist sentiments. They were important because their decisions could certainly affect the outcome of the war.

Delaware was never in doubt, but secessionists were strong in parts of Maryland, and Lincoln sent Federal troops into the state to sway the public and the legislature. Fearing arrest if they voted for the South, Maryland's lawmakers passed resolutions supporting the Union.

Leonidas Polk

Kentucky was so evenly divided that the legislature voted to proclaim neutrality and forbade either the U.S. or the CSA to operate within its borders. Both governments respected Kentucky's neutrality at first, but put troops just outside its borders to keep the other side from moving in. Grant sent several regiments of troops to Cairo, Illinois, on the Ohio River. *Leonidas Polk* feared Grant would enter Kentucky to take the bluffs along the river, so he occupied the spot himself. Because the South had broken the state's neutrality, the Kentucky legislature invited the Federals in to drive the Rebels out. Grant moved in, occupying Paducah and Southland at the mouths of the Tennessee and Cumberland Rivers.

To hold Kentucky and protect Tennessee, *A.S. Johnston* was ordered to direct southern operations in the state. Federal forces in Kentucky were divided between Don Carlos Buell and Henry Halleck. In January 1862, CSA forces were defeated at Mill Springs and withdrew into Tennessee. Kentucky did not secede, but furnished 35,000 soldiers to the South.

Missourians had argued over North-South issues. When the Civil War began, Governor Claiborne Jackson refused Lincoln's call for troops and tried to seize the U.S. arsenal at St. Louis. Captain Nathaniel Lyon, commander at the arsenal, shipped ammunition and 60,000 muskets to Illinois for safekeeping. In May 1861, he captured a pro-southern militia camp and marched his prisoners to St. Louis. That provoked rioting that killed 31 civilians and two soldiers.

Former governor *Sterling Price* recruited pro-southern state guard units for the Confederacy. On August 10, 1861, Lyon attacked *Price's* camp at Wilson's Creek. Lyon was killed, and *Price* drove Union forces back toward Jefferson City. Guerilla warfare broke out all over the state. On September 20, *Price* defeated Federal troops at Lexington, leaving southwest Missouri open to southern occupation.

In November 1861, Lincoln appointed Henry Halleck as commander of the new Department of the Missouri, which included western Kentucky. By then, *Price* was under the command of *Earl Van Dorn,* who planned to build a large army and capture St. Louis. Halleck sent Samuel Curtis to attack *Van Dorn* at Pea Ridge, Arkansas. The Federal victory there on March 7 and 8, 1862, kept Missouri in the Union, but did not prevent 30,000 Missourians from fighting in the Confederate army.

Name _____

Class _____

POINTS TO CONSIDER

1. What would have happened if all the border states had joined the CSA?

_____

_____

_____

_____

_____

2. Was it a good idea for Polk to enter Kentucky and break the state's neutrality?

_____

_____

_____

_____

3. Since the border states contributed many men to the South, do you think it really mattered whether they officially seceded or not? Explain your answer.

_____

_____

_____

_____

Name _____

Class _____

CHALLENGES

1. Why was border state support important to both sides?

_____

_____

2. How did Lincoln keep Maryland in the Union?

_____

_____

3. How did Kentucky try to stay out of the war?

_____

4. Who was the first general to move troops into Kentucky?

_____

5. What Kentucky towns did Grant occupy?

_____

6. What CSA general was ordered to hold Kentucky and protect Tennessee?

_____

7. How many Kentucky men served in the Confederate army?

_____

8. How did Governor Claiborne Jackson of Missouri respond when Lincoln asked for troops?

_____

_____

9. Which general won at Wilson's Creek and Lexington, Missouri?

_____

10. What Union victory prevented Missouri from going to the Confederacy?

_____

THE BATTLE AT SHILOH CHURCH

Albert Sydney Johnston

After victories at Forts Henry and Donelson, the Federal commanders were sure that the next battle would come whenever they chose. The CSA commander, *Albert Johnston,* withdrew to Corinth, Mississippi, and kept tabs on Grant's activities. Reports of more Federal troops arriving and Don Carlos Buell's troops on the way were disturbing to *Johnston* and his second in command, recently arrived *P.G.T. Beauregard.* One element was in their favor: the Federals were making no effort to prepare defenses. With a force of 40,000 men, many of them raw recruits, *Johnston* decided to hit Grant before the Yankees united their forces.

The Confederate march north was slow and far too noisy to suit *Beauregard*, who tried to persuade *Johnston* to call off the attack, but *Johnston* had made up his mind to go through with it. During the night of April 4-5, 1862, the two armies made their first contact, but William T. Sherman still saw no reason to fear a full scale enemy attack.

On April 6, the Rebel forces hit troops of Sherman and Ben Prentiss, forcing them back. But in the thick woods and small clearings, it was impossible for the southern forces to remain organized. Their strongest resistance came from Federals hidden on a sunken road that was given the nickname of the "Hornet's Nest." Grant was seven miles away, at Savannah, when he heard the guns roaring that morning, and he took a steamboat to Pittsburg Landing where he took charge of the situation. Prentiss was told to hold the Hornet's Nest at all cost.

That afternoon, *Johnston* received a leg wound he hardly noticed, but it had severed an artery, and he died soon afterward. Now, *Beauregard* was in command at a time when his troops were driving the Yankees back to the landing. However, Grant's defense was strengthened by a strong combination of artillery and gunboats. At 6 p.m., to the dismay of his troops, *Beauregard* called off operations for the day. It was a big mistake. During the night, Buell's 20,000 bluecoats arrived, and the 20,000 reinforcements *Beauregard* expected from *Earl Van Dorn* did not.

It rained hard that night, and the roar of Federal cannons added to the misery of the Rebels. The Yankee attack began early in the morning, and *Beauregard's* troops were pushed back. Then they rallied and pushed the bluecoats back to the Peach Orchard. When he learned *Van Dorn* had been held up in crossing the Mississippi, *Beauregard* began to withdraw. The Union soldiers were as worn out as his and made little effort to follow. Some attempt was made to pursue the graycoats on the 8th, but *Nathan Forrest's* cavalry attacked and discouraged any further pursuit.

There were major failures in leadership on both sides; both generals received much criticism from their nation's press. For the troops, it was an unforgettable experience, as they had participated in the largest battle ever fought (to that time) on American soil. Casualties were high: 3,400 men dead and 16,000 wounded. Grant later said: "It was a high price to pay for a country church and steamboat dock."

Name _____

Class _____

POINTS TO CONSIDER

1. If you had been on Johnston's staff in early April 1862, would you have advised him to attack? Why or why not?

_____

_____

_____

_____

_____

2. The area around Shiloh Church was heavily wooded with little cleared patches. What problems do you think this would have caused for troops of both armies?

_____

_____

_____

_____

_____

3. As a reporter critical of the way the battle had been conducted, what would you have written about either Grant or Beauregard?

_____

_____

_____

_____

_____

Name _____

Class _____

CHALLENGES

1. Who was the CSA commander with headquarters at Corinth, Mississippi?

_____

2. Why did Johnston decide to attack the Yankee forces gathering near Shiloh Church?

_____

_____

3. Who commanded the Union troops that were first attacked on April 6?

_____

4. What nickname was given to the sunken road?

_____

5. What general was killed the afternoon of April 6? _____

Who took charge? _____

6. Which army received reinforcements that night?

_____

7. Why did Beauregard decide to withdraw?

_____

_____

8. Who discouraged Union troops from attempting to attack the retreating Confederates?

_____

9. How many were killed at Shiloh?

_____

10. How many were wounded?

_____

A HOT DAY AT ANTIETAM CREEK

**Burnside's Bridge, Antietam Creek, Maryland
September 1862**

In September 1862, *Robert E. Lee* began a campaign he hoped would take his army into Maryland and Pennsylvania. From there, he could strike at Philadelphia, Baltimore, or even Washington. If the drive was successful, the South might receive recognition by France and England and perhaps financial aid from one or both.

Lee's army entered Maryland September 5 and pushed toward Frederick. There, on September 9, he issued Special Order 191, dividing his army. He sent *Jackson* to capture Harpers Ferry, while the main force moved toward Hagerstown. An officer carelessly wrapped the order around three cigars, and it was found by Federal soldiers who took it to McClellan on the 13th. With an army outnumbering *Lee's* by 36,000 men, and knowing that the opponent's army was split, most generals would have moved quickly to take advantage of the situation. But McClellan did not, partly because he feared this was a trap to pull him away from Washington so another Confederate army could attack the capital.

Finally, the next day, the two armies clashed at South Mountain, and the Confederates were pushed back. However, *Jackson* was successful in capturing Harpers Ferry on the 15th. When *Lee* learned of that victory later in the day, he decided to make his stand at Antietam Creek. With only 19,000 men on hand, the Potomac River at his back, and 40,000 men on the way to join him, *Lee* counted on McClellan to delay action, and he did. As McClellan planned the battle, his men would attack the Confederate left, then the right, and the reserves would be used to support either attack, or hit the Confederate center if *Lee* weakened it to support troops on either wing.

September 17, action began with a fury when Joe Hooker and Joe Mansfield's troops attacked the 12,000 Confederates under *John Hood* hidden in a cornfield north of Sharpsburg. At first, the Yankees pushed the Rebels back, but then *Hood's* men retook the field, only to be met by fresh troops who forced them back again. In two hours of bitter fighting, Mansfield was killed, Hooker wounded, and the field littered with the dead and wounded.

The next focus of attention was the center where Edwin "Bull Head" Sumner's troops charged toward *D.H. Hill's* troops hidden in a sunken road. The Rebels held the road for three hours, and then Yankees overcame them; this piece of land would afterward be known as the "Bloody Lane." Now there was no Confederate center, but McClellan refused to send more troops into the area, fearing that this was a trap.

On the Confederate right, Ambrose Burnside had been busy trying to move troops across a stone bridge (Burnside's Bridge) and finally was able to overcome *Longstreet's* resistance. At the moment when it appeared victory was at hand, *A.P. Hill's* division arrived from Harpers Ferry and stopped Burnside in his tracks.

It had been a long day with 4,100 dead and 18,500 more wounded in the most bloody day of the war. *Lee* expected McClellan to attack the next day, but when he did not, *Lee* crossed the Potomac. Lincoln fired McClellan for the second time.

 *Southern military leaders are in italics.

Name _____

Class _____

POINTS TO CONSIDER

1. What difference would it make for Lee's army to be fighting in Maryland rather than in their usual area in Virginia?

_____

_____

_____

_____

2. What does the way Lee fought this battle tell you about his attitude toward McClellan's abilities?

_____

_____

_____

_____

3. If you were Lincoln, would you see this as a victory or a disappointment? Why?

_____

_____

_____

_____

Name_____

Class_____

CHALLENGES

1. What did the South have to gain from marching into Maryland?

_____

_____

2. How did McClellan learn about Special Order 191?

_____

_____

3. How many more men did McClellan have than Lee?

_____

4. Why was Jackson away from the army when the battle took place at South Mountain?

_____

_____

5. Where did Hooker's men clash with Hood's?

_____

6. What Union general was killed in that encounter?

_____

7. By what name is the sunken road known today?

_____

8. How did "Burnside's Bridge" get its name?

_____

9. Who stopped Burnside's advance?

_____

10. How many were killed at Antietam? _____

Wounded?_____

MEDICAL CARE IN THE CIVIL WAR

Nowhere was the lack of preparation for war more obvious than in the field of medicine. When the war began, the U.S. army had 115 medical officers, 22 of whom resigned to join the Confederate army. Politics plagued the U.S. Medical Department. Three surgeon generals were fired between 1861 and 1863; then Joseph Barnes took over the office and remained there until the end of the war. He saw the department expand to over 10,000 medical men. The South had no such political problems.

Headquarters of the U.S. Sanitary Commission, Brandy Station, November 1863

Samuel Moore served as the CSA surgeon general through the whole war. With resources very limited, he performed near-miracles. Unfortunately, when Richmond fell, the records of the CSA medical department were destroyed, so little is known about how the department was organized.

Both medical departments faced enormous challenges. Neither the U.S. nor CSA were experienced in handling large numbers of men in the field. Camp hygiene was so lacking that diseases spread through both armies. Of the 360,000 Federals who died in war, 31 percent died of battle wounds and 69 percent of disease. Medical officers in both armies blamed health problems on spoiled food, polluted water, bad hygiene, infection from lice and fleas, and contagious diseases recruits brought to camp. The most common diseases were measles, mumps, and rheumatism. Cures for these and other diseases did not come until later.

Early in the war, wounded men were sheltered in schools, churches, barns, and even chicken houses near the battlefield. There were no organized field hospitals until the U.S. army set one up at Shiloh in April 1862. There were no ambulances early in the war, and if a wounded man got to the surgeon, someone had to carry him there. Late in the war, horse-drawn ambulances were available to move the wounded.

Amputation was the usual cure for most wounded soldiers. Working quickly to prevent gangrene, surgeons cut off arms and legs, but then didn't bother to clean saws and other instruments between operations.

Eventually, a system emerged featuring dressing stations on the battlefield where the wounded man's wound was dressed. He was then sent to a hospital area in the rear. From there, he was either discharged or sent back to his unit. Women worked in these permanent hospitals. Female nurses were popular among patients, who longed for their gentle touch and soft words of comfort. A civilian organization, the U.S. Sanitary Commission, also supplied nurses to general hospitals. In the South, the Women's Relief Society sent volunteers to bathe, bandage, and comfort.

Both sides had a shortage of hospitals. New ones were built, and other existing buildings (at colleges, warehouses, hotels, and railroad depots) were converted. The Chimborazo at Richmond was the largest during the war, and 76,000 men were treated there. The second largest was Lincoln, in Washington, which treated 46,000 men.

73

Name _____

Class _____

POINTS TO CONSIDER

1. How would a modern doctor feel if he had to work under the conditions that a Civil War doctor did?

_____

_____

_____

_____

_____

2. Why do you think that in the Civil War there was a much larger percentage killed than injured, while in modern wars, we have had many more injured than killed?

_____

_____

_____

_____

3. What simple measures might have been taken that would have saved the lives of many of those who died?

_____

_____

_____

_____

Name _____

Class _____

CHALLENGES

1. How many medical men did the U.S. army have when the war began? _____

How many of those joined the Confederate army? _____

2. How many wore the title of "surgeon general" in the Union army during the war?

_____

3. Why is so little known about the CSA Medical Corps?

_____

_____

4. What was the leading cause of death in the Civil War?

_____

5. What were the most common contagious diseases in military camps during the war?

_____

6. What kinds of places were used as field hospitals in the war?

_____

7. Where did the army first set up a field hospital?

_____

8. What was the most common method of treating a battlefield wound?

_____

9. What civilian agency supplied many nurses for the Union army?

_____

10. What was the largest hospital in the Civil War? _____

Where was it located? _____

FREDERICKSBURG: A CHRISTMAS PRESENT FOR LEE

Pontoon Bridge across the Rappahannock River, Fredericksburg, Virginia

Lincoln had tolerated McClellan for over a year. He had ordered, pleaded, and coaxed "Little Mac" to use the Army of the Potomac to its fullest and defeat *Lee* once and for all. Finally, after McClellan's failure to chase the Confederates after the battle at Antietam, Lincoln had had enough. In November 1862, McClellan was fired and replaced by Ambrose Burnside.

The North demanded action. Burnside responded with a plan to take Fredericksburg, Virginia, on the Rappahannock River, then drive on to Richmond. The plan was simple and obvious. It depended on taking Fredericksburg before *Lee* caught on to what was happening.

Lee's army had been rebuilt since Antietam. He now had 72,000 men in two corps under *Stonewall Jackson* and *James Longstreet*. Burnside's army consisted of 106,000 men led by Edwin Sumner, Joe Hooker, and William Franklin. Burnside's troops began moving forward in mid-November and encamped across from Fredericksburg. They were spotted by Confederate cavalry, and *Lee* sent *Longstreet* to Fredericksburg to keep an eye on them. Convinced a big battle was in the making, *Lee's* whole army went to Fredericksburg. The Federals' element of surprise was gone.

Burnside's plan depended on pontoon bridges to cross the river, but red tape and bungling had sent them elsewhere. Burnside fumed until the pontoons were delivered two weeks later. Meanwhile, the Confederates were busy building defenses and making plans.

A crescent-shaped line of hills ran around Fredericksburg. *Lee's* troops took up positions on Telegraph Hill, Marye's Heights, and Taylor's Hill. *Stuart's* cavalry was posted between these hills and the river, and only one brigade was located in the town. At the foot of Marye's Heights was a sunken road, protected by a stone wall. *Longstreet* placed 2,500 riflemen there. *Lee* waited for Burnside to make his crossing and walk into the trap.

Finally, Burnside's pontoons arrived, and engineers went to work on assembling the bridges. Union troops began crossing the river on the bridges while nature pelted them with snow, sleet, and freezing winds. On December 13, a heavy fog lifted at midmorning and Burnside's long-delayed attack began.

George Meade struck *Jackson's* position south of town, but was stopped by *Jubal Early* and *A.P. Hill*. In town, Sumner's and Hooker's men came forward in parade formation and were mowed down. Seven attempts were made to reach the sunken road, and the bodies continued to pile up in front of the wall. Watching from Marye's Heights, *Lee* commented: "It is well that war is so terrible—we should grow too fond of it."

During the night, wounded men lay in ice and snow while their blood froze in pools on the cold ground. Burnside wanted to continue the battle, but his officers argued strongly against it, and they prevailed. The southern generals were disappointed when they found the Yankees had pulled back. Burnside's failure cost him his job, and 12,700 of his men lost their lives or were severely wounded.

76 *Southern military leaders are in italics.

Name _____

Class _____

POINTS TO CONSIDER

1. What do you think caused Burnside to go ahead with the attack even though he knew the Confederates were on to his plan?

_____

_____

_____

_____

2. What did Lee mean by his remark about warfare?

_____

_____

_____

_____

3. As a journalist covering the battle, what adjectives might you use to describe the Union soldiers who attacked Marye's Heights? What might you use to describe Burnside?

_____

_____

_____

_____

Name _____

Class _____

CHALLENGES

1. Whom did Burnside replace?

_____

2. On what river was Fredericksburg located?

_____

3. Who were the principal commanders under Lee?

_____

4. Who were Burnside's principal commanders?

_____

5. What delayed Burnside's crossing of the river?

_____

_____

6. Where did Longstreet place his riflemen at Marye's Heights?

_____

7. What added to the misery of Union soldiers crossing the river?

_____

8. How many times were the Federals beaten back in their attack on Marye's Heights?

_____

9. Who wanted to continue the attack on the 14th?

_____

10. Confederate casualties at Fredericksburg numbered 5,300. How many more Union soldiers were killed or wounded than southern?

_____

THE DRAFT IS IMPOSED: SOUTH AND NORTH

Horatio Seymour

After the first rush to join the army, there was a noticeable drop in enlistments on both sides. This could be partly blamed on marching and drilling, poor food, uncomfortable tents, and sergeants and officers who yelled at recruits. Stories of battles, death, and wounds also discouraged the faint-hearted. If men did not choose to fight, new means had to be found to fill the ranks of the army and protect the nation.

The South was first to adopt the draft. In April 1862, it required military service of men from ages 18 to 35. Five months later, the upper age was set at 45, and in 1864, it included those from 17 to 50. There were exceptions. Certain professions and occupations were excluded, a man could hire a substitute, and one exemption would be granted to every master or overseer of every 20 slaves. Since teachers and druggists were exempt, many men entered those professions. In some parts of the South, especially mountain regions, it required great effort to catch draft dodgers, who saw no advantage in fighting to preserve slavery for the rich. By 1863, ads offering $6,000 for an acceptable substitute appeared in newspapers. Because of desertions and losses to disease, the South's manpower supply was so reduced that General *Patrick Cleburne* suggested using slaves in the army. General *Lee* lent his support to that idea in January 1865; the bill passed in March, but the war ended before blacks fought for the CSA.

The Union draft law was as unpopular as the South's. Passed in March 1863, it included able-bodied men between 20-45 years of age for service not to exceed three years. There were exemptions allowed, including some professions, those who hired substitutes, or those who paid the government $300. In both North and South, those subject to the draft complained this was a "rich man's war and a poor man's fight."

Communities reacted differently to the draft. A riot began in New York City that lasted from July 13-17, 1863. The hoodlum element in the city, drunk and savage, attacked blacks on the streets, looted stores, burned the Orphan Asylum for Colored Children, and shoved aside anyone trying to stop them. The mayor asked the governor for help, and on the second day of the riot, Governor Horatio Seymour arrived. Addressing the mob as "My friends," he tried to quiet them by saying an aide had been sent to President Lincoln urging him to call off the draft.

Many northern counties faced a problem. They did not want to draft men; that made the county look unpatriotic and turned voters against the local officials. Their problem was solved by a "bounty broker," who promised county officials he could find enough men for the quota. He found most recruits in bars; after getting the men drunk, the broker turned them over to a recruiting sergeant. They also found underage boys. Brokers had a woman who claimed she was the boy's mother sign his enlistment papers. They took old men, put boot black on their hair, and claimed they were much younger. Very few good men were brought into the army by brokers.

79 * Southern military leaders are in italics.

Name _____

Class _____

POINTS TO CONSIDER

1. As a poor northern man at the time of the Civil War, what would you think about the draft? Why?

_____

_____

_____

_____

_____

2. As a southern white man who was a small farmer at the time of the Civil War, what would you think about the draft? Why?

_____

_____

_____

_____

_____

3. Do you think Governor Seymour should have reacted differently when facing the rioters? Give reasons to support your position.

_____

_____

_____

_____

Name _____

Class _____

CHALLENGES

1. What were the age limits on the first Confederate draft?

_____

2. In 1864, what age limits were included in the Confederate draft?

_____

3. Why was the 20-slave exemption unpopular?

_____

_____

4. How much were southerners offering substitutes by 1863?

_____

5. What new group could be enlisted in the CSA army in 1865?

_____

6. A northern man would have to pay how much to buy an exemption from the government?

_____

7. What was the age limit set for the Union draft in 1863?

_____

8. What northern city had a draft riot?

_____

9. Why did counties hire bounty brokers?

_____

_____

10. Would you say brokers brought good or poor quality men into the army?

_____

THE *TRENT* AFFAIR: TEMPTING ENGLAND

Charles Wilkes

The last thing that Lincoln wanted was the very thing on Captain Charles Wilkes's mind when he spotted the mail packet *Trent* as it left Cuba on its way to England. On board that small ship were James Mason and John Slidell, two CSA diplomats on their way to England and France. Without asking permission, Wilkes decided, on his own, to capture them. His ship, the *San Jacinto,* fired a shot across the bow of the *Trent* on November 9, 1861. The boarding party he sent ordered the *Trent's* captain to turn the southerners over to them. The captain protested, but there was little he could do, and Mason and Slidell were taken away to a Boston prison.

Many in the North gave Wilkes celebrity status for what he had done, but Lincoln did not. He had created a diplomatic mess for Lincoln and Seward to clean up. The problem was that many important people in England favored the South and used this incident as a reason for backing the CSA. Southern supporters included those who: 1) thought the U.S. threatened England's top position in the world; a split U.S. would reduce that threat, 2) believed the South produced real gentlemen, while northerners were crude money worshipers, and 3) feared that the poor in England would be encouraged by a northern victory to demand the vote.

Fortunately for the Union, many in England favored the North. They had read *Uncle Tom's Cabin* and saw the war as a way to end slavery. There was also a need for American farm products because of crop failures in England. A leader of British factory workers, John Bright, kept in close touch with Lincoln, so Lincoln knew that the English factory workers believed a northern victory was important in their struggle for the vote. Of those who favored the North, the most important were Queen Victoria and her husband, Prince Albert.

When word reached England that Americans had stopped a British ship and took off two passengers, the British Foreign Office prepared a strong protest. Prince Albert saw the message and persuaded the Foreign Office to tone it down. The British demanded that Mason and Slidell be released and that the U.S. apologize "for the insult offered to the British flag."

What difference did the English attitude make? Their navy was the most powerful in the world, and if England chose, its ships could easily break the Union blockade. With British help, the Confederacy would win its independence. Leaders on both sides of the Atlantic realized the dangers of the situation.

Seward assured the English that Wilkes had acted on his own, without receiving any kind of approval. Since his action was improper, Mason and Slidell would be "cheerfully liberated." The two Confederates were released and, after they arrived in England, were ignored. Wilkes had almost done what Mason and Slidell could never have done on their own.

Name _____

Class _____

POINTS TO CONSIDER

1. A "loose cannon" is a person whose actions endanger others. In your view, was Wilkes a "loose cannon"?

_____

_____

_____

_____

_____

2. As an English supporter of the South, what kind of letter would you write to an English newspaper after you learned of the *Trent* affair?

_____

_____

_____

_____

3. Wilkes was promoted to Commodore in 1862. In light of what had happened in 1861, what do you make of that?

_____

_____

_____

_____

Name _____

Class _____

CHALLENGES

1. What type of ship was the *Trent?*

_____

2. Who were the two diplomats on board?

_____

3. Who was captain of the *San Jacinto?*

_____

4. How did the *Trent's* captain react when he was ordered to turn the two Confederates over to the Americans?

_____

5. Why did some English see a southern victory as helpful to England?

_____

_____

6. What spokesman for British factory workers had close connections with Lincoln?

_____

7. Who persuaded the Foreign Office to change the wording of their demands?

_____

8. What were the two demands?

_____

_____

9. Did the U.S. release the prisoners?

_____

10. What did they accomplish in England and France?

_____

CONGRESS CREATES A NEW FUTURE FOR THE NATION

Clement Vallandigham

When one thinks about the Civil War, one may think about generals and battles, but seldom of Congress. The reason is that Lincoln took Congress out of decision making about the war before Congress met in July 1861. By then, he had called up 75,000 volunteers, blockaded the southern coastline, and borrowed money to pay the costs. When Congress finally met, he asked their approval for what had already been done. They had little choice except to go along with him. Lincoln had made it clear that when it came to the war, he was the one in charge.

Congress was reluctant to let Lincoln have so much power and kept an eagle eye on him. Radical Republicans thought Lincoln was too easy on the South. They pushed to create the Joint Committee on the Conduct of the War, which investigated generals and often embarrassed Lincoln. Most Democrats said he was not doing enough to make peace. One of these, Representative Clement Vallandigham, said the war was "wicked, cruel and unnecessary." He was arrested by General Burnside for that remark. With the war going badly, most in Congress willingly let Lincoln take over and take the blame.

Republicans in Congress remembered how southern Democrats had always blocked their proposals to raise the tariff (taxes on imports), give government land to farmers (homesteads), and build a railroad from the North to California. With Republicans in control of the White House and Congress, the time was right for them to fulfill the campaign promises of the 1860 platform.

The first change was to increase taxes. The Federal government had never spent money as quickly as it was now, so Congress raised the tariff in 1861 (Morrill Tariff), put a special tax on the sale of some luxuries (excise tax), and even added an income tax. With government expenses far higher than income, the government began selling bonds. They were still so short on cash that the "greenback" was issued. This was paper money that people could use to pay debts, but it was backed only by faith in the government. If battles were being lost, greenback value dropped. When battles were won, the value went up. Debate over greenbacks went on for years.

In May 1862, Congress passed the Homestead Act, which allowed any citizen (or person intending to become a citizen) to settle on 160 acres of government land. After living there five years, the land would be the homesteader's to keep.

Congress also chartered two railroads in 1862: the Union Pacific (UP), which was to build west from Omaha, and the Central Pacific (CP) to build east from Sacramento. In 1864, Congress chartered the Northern Pacific (NP) to be built from Lake Superior to Portland, Oregon. When the war ended and thousands of unemployed veterans were eager to find work, construction moved forward quickly. In 1869, the CP and UP met at Promontory Point, Utah, and one could travel from the Atlantic to the Pacific by rail.

Name _____

Class _____

POINTS TO CONSIDER

1. Do you think Congress, rather than Lincoln, should have selected generals? Give reasons for your position.

_____

_____

_____

_____

_____

2. Why would the Homestead Act be useful to soldiers after the war?

_____

_____

_____

_____

_____

3. How did the Homestead Act and railroad construction play a major part in settling the West?

_____

_____

_____

_____

_____

Name _____

Class _____

CHALLENGES

1. Who was behind creating the Joint Committee on the Conduct of the War?

_____

2. Who was an example of a Peace Democrat?

_____

3. Who ordered him to be arrested?

_____

4. Did the Morrill Tariff raise or lower taxes on imports?

_____

5. What is an excise tax?

_____

6. What nickname was given to the paper money Congress issued?

_____

7. How much land could a homesteader receive under the 1862 law?

_____

8. How long did he have to wait before he could receive the land at no cost?

_____

9. What railroad built east from Sacramento?

_____

What railroad built west from Omaha?

_____

10. Where was the Northern Pacific built?

_____

ENTERTAINMENT DURING THE WAR

For both the soldier and civilian, war is hard on the nerves. In such times, people need something to take their minds off their problems. Men in uniform think about their relatives, friends, and girl friends. Civil War soldiers were hard on the outside, but were both sentimental *and* playful.

During the war, reading became more popular in the North. Serious materials like Charles Dickens's novels or poetry by Alfred Lord Tennyson or Henry Wadsworth Longfellow had many readers. Magazines

During their free time, soldiers might take time to read or pose for a picture.

like *Harper's Weekly, Atlantic Monthly,* and *Godey's Lady's Book* increased circulation. Newspapers carrying the latest news from the war were grabbed up almost before the print was dry. For men interested in more spicy reading, there was the *Police Gazette.* "Dime novels," cheap paperbacks written very quickly by Erastus Beadle or an imitator, were read in secret. The South was short on paper, and there, even newspapers became scarce.

Northern soldiers passing through New York, like other tourists, liked to stop by P.T. Barnum's American Museum to see General Tom Thumb perform.

Southerners had more trouble finding joy in life when food was scarce, clothes wore out, and news from the war was discouraging. In cities, theaters were very popular. Entertainers drew large crowds. A black pianist, "Blind Tom," traveled from one town to another, as did jugglers, organ grinders, and other performers. Social rules changed, and it became quite acceptable for a lady to converse with a man and dance with a stranger.

Music was very popular on both sides and was used to build morale in the armies. General *Lee* said: "It is impossible to have an army without music," and after a bad defeat, General Hancock ordered every band to play "The Battle Cry of Freedom." Over 9,000 songs were written in the North during the war, but less than 100 ever became "hits." Patriotic songs of the North included "Battle Hymn of the Republic" "Battle Cry of Freedom," and "Marching Through Georgia." Southern soldiers liked "Dixie," "Bonnie Blue Flag," and "Maryland, My Maryland." Sentimental songs were popular with both armies: "The Last Rose of Summer," "Home, Sweet Home," "Annie Laurie," and "Lorena" were among the most popular. Hymns like "Rock of Ages" and "Nearer My God to Thee" were also favorites around campfires.

Athletic events were popular in army camps: wrestling, lifting, boxing, and baseball among them. The modern fan would find baseball has changed since the 1860s. Home plate was round, the pitcher stood 45 feet away, and he delivered underhand and stiff-armed. There were no bases on balls, but if the batter failed to strike at good balls, the umpire could call a strike.

The Great Snowball Fight occurred when Tennessee and Georgia soldiers under General *Joe Johnston* took advantage of a heavy snowfall at Dalton, Georgia. The men formed in ranks and, led by officers on horseback, charged each other's lines. The battle eventually involved 5,000 soldiers and ended with none killed and only black eyes and a few broken bones for the injured.

88   * Southern military leaders are in italics.

Name _____

Class _____

POINTS TO CONSIDER

1. If a modern war of great size were to take place, how would the modern soldier probably imitate the Civil War soldier when it came to entertainment?

_____

_____

_____

_____

_____

2. What kind of music do you think would be popular in a major modern war?

_____

_____

_____

_____

_____

3. Do you think men are sentimental today? Give some reasons for your opinion.

_____

_____

_____

_____

_____

Name _____

Class _____

CHALLENGES

1. Who were two of the favorite poets of the Civil War era?

_____

2. What magazine did men read if their mothers were not around?

_____

3. What writer was famous for "dime novels" at the time?

_____

4. Who was one of the star performers at the American Museum?

_____

5. What black performer had successful tours of the South?

_____

6. What Union patriotic song is best known today?

_____

7. What Confederate patriotic song is best known today?

_____

8. In baseball, how far did the pitcher stand from home plate?

_____

9. How was home plate different during the Civil War than it is now?

_____

10. How many men took part in the Great Snowball Fight?

_____

CIVILIANS DO THEIR PART IN THE WAR

Dr. Mary Walker was awarded the Congressional Medal of Honor.

It is in the nature of modern warfare that civilians become involved, whether they want to or not. Wilmer McLean, a farmer at Bull Run, became part of the Civil War when the first battle of the war was fought on his land. He had enough of that and moved his family to Appomattox. Others like him saw armies moving past their farms and through their towns and hoped no one would stop long enough to have a battle or loot a house. Many came out to cheer their troops and brought buckets of cool water fresh from the well. Volunteers were going to play a big part in the war.

Some acted as spies. Rose Greenhow was acquainted with many government officials and used her sources to help Beauregard at Bull Run. Belle Boyd became the most famous Confederate spy, sending information and medicine to help Jackson's army. Keeping a watchful eye on Confederates was the Pinkerton Detective Agency's assignment during the war. Elizabeth Van Lew and her former slave, Mary Bowser, provided useful information for Grant from their home in Richmond. Many who were never known kept leaders informed on the movement of enemy armies.

The role of the battlefield nurse had been made noble by Florence Nightingale during the Crimean War, but the Civil War also produced "angels of the battlefield." Lincoln gave Dorothea Dix the title of "Superintendent of U.S. Army Nurses," and even though she had faults in her methods of doing her job, she was successful in enlisting public support. She asked the public for canned goods and night shirts, and more were given than the army needed. Clara Barton, later famous as head of the American Red Cross, served as a battlefield nurse during the war and wore the title of "Superintendent of Nurses for the Army of the James." "Mother" Mary Bickerdyke became a hero to many wounded enlisted men and did much to improve the quality of their care. Dr. Mary Walker became an assistant surgeon for the army, and even though she was a civilian, she was awarded the Congressional Medal of Honor.

Voluntary organizations organized to meet special needs. The U.S. Sanitary Commission raised money through "Sanitary Fairs" for a program to supply food, clothing, bandages, and medicine for the troops.

The YMCA and Protestant ministers formed the Christian Commission to provide nursing care, blankets, and medicine to wounded soldiers. The Catholic Sisters of Charity supplied nurses to army hospitals. Many individuals, churches, and communities helped traveling soldiers with a place to stop, rest, and talk. Untold hours of work by women wrapping bandages and preparing jelly or meals for the troops helped provide some reminder of home to men far away from loved ones.

The unsung heroes were those women and children who plowed the land, milked the cows, and repaired fences, so that fathers, husbands, and sons could go into the army and serve their nation with a clear conscience.

Name _____

Class _____

POINTS TO CONSIDER

1. Why were women more successful as spies than men?

_____

_____

_____

_____

_____

2. Nursing was still very new in the 1860s. Why did nurses catch so much criticism from doctors at the time?

_____

_____

_____

_____

3. If civilians had not become involved, what difference would it have made in the lives of the soldiers?

_____

_____

_____

_____

Name _____

Class _____

CHALLENGES

1. What spy helped Beauregard at Bull Run?

_____

2. What spy helped Jackson?

_____

3. Name two Union spies in Richmond.

_____

4. Which detective agency was hired to keep an eye on Confederate agents?

_____

5. Who was U.S. Superintendent of Nurses?

_____

6. Which Civil War nurse became head of the American Red Cross later?

_____

7. Who was the first woman to receive the Congressional Medal of Honor?

_____

8. What group used fairs to raise funds?

_____

9. What group was formed by Protestant ministers and the YMCA?

_____

10. What did the Sisters of Charity supply?

_____

CIVIL RIGHTS IN THE NORTH DURING THE WAR

Imagine that you are walking down the street one day, and a policeman grabs you and takes you to jail. No one tells you why you are being held, and the police never take your case to court. You could sit there for years, unless you were protected by *habeas corpus.* It gives you the right to go to court and have the charges against you read. The Constitution guarantees that right (Article 1, Section 9) except "when in cases of rebellion or invasion the public safety may require it."

Roger B. Taney

Now imagine you are Lincoln. Eight days ago, troops marching through Baltimore were attacked by mobs throwing bricks and stones. In that fight, twelve civilians and four soldiers were killed. So many Maryland railroad bridges were burned and telegraph lines cut that Washington is cut off from the rest of the North.

On April 27, 1861, you decide that the emergency requires that the writ of habeas corpus is to be suspended in the area from Washington to Philadelphia. Anyone arrested by military authorities may be held without trial.

John Merryman is a secessionist accused of burning bridges and cutting telegraph lines; he is arrested and taken to Ft. McHenry. His lawyer says Merryman has a right to go to court and takes his appeal to the circuit court. The Chief Judge of the circuit is Roger Taney, the U.S. Supreme Court's chief justice. He issues a writ of habeas corpus, but the fort's commander refuses to bring Merryman to court. Taney writes that Lincoln has no authority to suspend the writ, since Article 1 deals with powers of Congress, not the president; Taney says the Constitution does not permit a citizen to be held without a trial. Seven weeks later, Merryman is released and is to be tried in circuit court, but the government never brings the case to court because it knows no Maryland jury would convict Merryman.

If a newspaper was believed disloyal, the army might arrest the editor and hold him for a few days. Another method was to refuse to allow the papers to be mailed. The postmaster-general justified that policy by saying that a newspaper cannot aim blows at the government and the Union, then claim their protection. Mail cannot be used for the government's destruction.

Quakers were opposed to war, but all except one had paid $300 to the government or hired a substitute. The exception was Cyrus Pringle, who refused to do either of those, but when drafted, he refused to obey any orders. His situation came to Lincoln's attention, and he ordered the man sent home. In 1864, the War Department made a policy that religious objectors were to be used in hospitals, or take care of freedmen, or pay $300 for the care of sick and wounded soldiers.

The case of *Ex Parte Milligan* was decided after the war ended. Arrested in 1864, Milligan was sentenced to be hanged by a military court. He appealed to the Supreme Court, which ruled in 1866 that the president could not try civilians in military courts where regular courts were operating.

Name _____

Class _____

POINTS TO CONSIDER

1. Do you think that freedom of speech and press should be more limited during a war than under usual situations? Why or why not?

_____

_____

_____

_____

_____

2. What dangers to civil liberties were there in refusing to deliver anti-war newspapers in the mail?

_____

_____

_____

_____

_____

3. How should conscientious objectors be treated? Would you have approved of the policy adopted in 1864? Why or why not?

_____

_____

_____

_____

_____

Name _____

Class _____

CHALLENGES

1. Where is *habeas corpus* discussed in the Constitution?

_____

2. How does *habeas corpus* protect you?

_____

3. In what city were soldiers attacked in April 1861?

_____

4. Of what crime was John Merryman accused?

_____

5. What judge wanted to hear his case?

_____

6. What officer refused to let Merryman go to court?

_____

7. What two ways were used to deal with disloyal newspapers?

_____

_____

8. How did Lincoln solve the Pringle problem?

_____

9. How were religious objectors handled afterward?

_____

_____

10. After reading about the Milligan case, would you say the Court thought Lincoln was right in the Merryman case?

_____

FREEING THE BLACKS AND LETTING THEM FIGHT

Robert G. Shaw Memorial, showing the 54th Massachusetts Infantry Regiment.

One of the most troubling questions of the war was whether slaves should be freed, or when it should be done. In the early stages of the war, Congress said in early 1862 that the purpose of the war was to save the Union, not end slavery. That view was very close to Lincoln's. In August 1862, he answered criticism from Horace Greeley, editor of the *New York Tribune.* Lincoln replied that regardless of his personal wish that slavery end, "My paramount object in this struggle *is* to save the Union, and is *not* either to save or to destroy slavery." Lincoln's problem was that loyal border states like Missouri, Kentucky, and Maryland still had slaves; he could not risk stirring up more opposition in those states.

Northern opinion at the time was as divided as it could possibly be. The old abolitionists were sure that freeing slaves was right. Others said to free the blacks, but send them to Africa or Central America. Blacks opposed this idea, and one, Robert Purvis, bluntly told Lincoln: "Sir, this is our country as much as it is yours, and we will not leave it." Despite protests from blacks and abolitionists, Lincoln tried to establish a colony on an island near Haiti. It was a miserable failure, and after many of the black "colonists" became ill, the survivors were brought back.

There were some real legal questions with freeing slaves in loyal states. Amendment V of the Constitution says that private property cannot be taken without just compensation. Lincoln offered a deal to border state leaders: free your slaves, and the government will pay $400 for each one. They turned him down flat. If he could not persuade loyal border staters to free slaves, he could justify freeing Confederate slaves as a war measure. On September 22, 1862, he announced that on January 1, 1863, slaves in those states still at war with the U.S. would be freed. On that date, he issued the Emancipation Proclamation. It was not until 1865 and the 13th Amendment that all slavery in the U.S. was made a thing of the past.

The Emancipation Proclamation raised another question. Should blacks be enlisted in the army? Black leaders like Frederick Douglass pointed out that General Ben Butler was already using escaped slaves at Fortress Monroe to build defenses. They were given a shovel and pick for digging, a red shirt for their back, and a pistol for their belt. By early 1863, Lincoln was ready to accept blacks into the army. The Bureau of Colored Troops was created, and General Lorenzo Thomas was sent to the Mississippi Valley to recruit blacks. He was able to raise 76,000 black troops.

Black regiments were led by white officers, and less than 100 blacks ever became officers. Their enthusiasm ran high, and in battle they often suffered high casualties. In May 1863, black troops drove off a Confederate attack at Milliken's Bend, Mississippi. That July, the 54th Massachusetts proved itself as it attempted to take Ft. Wagner, South Carolina. Black soldiers could take pride in helping to make freedom a reality for those still held as slaves.

Name _____

Class _____

POINTS TO CONSIDER

1. It was easy for critics to want to rush Lincoln into freeing slaves. Why was it harder for him than it was for them?

_____

_____

_____

_____

_____

2. Black troops received less pay than whites, did harder work than whites, and were rarely promoted to officer. If you had been a black at the time, would those facts have caused you to not join the army?

_____

_____

_____

_____

_____

3. When blacks fought hard at Ft. Wagner, Milliken's Bend, Fort Pillow, and the Battle of the Crater, do you think that changed the public attitude toward them?

_____

_____

_____

_____

_____

Name _____

Class _____

CHALLENGES

1. In 1862, what did Congress think was the reason for the war?

_____

2. Why was Lincoln in no hurry to declare a policy ending slavery?

_____

_____

3. What did the abolitionists want Lincoln to do?

_____

4. What did Robert Purvis think of colonizing?

_____

5. How much did Lincoln offer to pay border state representatives for their slaves?

_____

6. How did they respond?

_____

7. When did the Emancipation Proclamation go into effect?

_____

8. Who was sent to recruit black troops in the Mississippi Valley?

_____

9. Name a battle in the West where blacks fought bravely.

_____

10. Name a battle in the East where the 54th Massachusetts fought bravely.

_____

CHANCELLORSVILLE: HOOKER'S LESSON IN WARFARE

Thomas "Stonewall" Jackson

After Burnside's crushing defeat at Fredericksburg, Lincoln again searched for a general to lead the Army of the Potomac. In January 1863, he chose "Fighting Joe" Hooker for the job, but doubted that he had the right man. He warned Hooker that the army had a defeatist spirit, and that would be a problem. He told Hooker not to be rash, but "with energy and sleepless vigilance go forward and give us victories."

Lee's army, on the other hand, had a confidence that ignored its ragged and hungry appearance. Despite the cold, the men enjoyed large snowball fights and waited for the Yankees to come back for another licking.

Hooker worked hard at rebuilding his army's confidence, and when Lincoln came out to see the army, he assured the president they were the "finest army on the planet" and would drive his way through to Richmond. Such boasting bothered Lincoln, who felt that defeating the enemy in battle was more important than capturing his capital.

Hooker began well, confusing the Confederates by moving at different points at the same time. The area involved was between Fredericksburg and Kelly's Ford, which crossed the Rappahannock River, a distance of about 15 miles. "Uncle John" Sedgwick was to threaten Fredericksburg, holding *Lee* there. Hooker would take 40,000 men west to Kelly's Ford. When Sedgwick's soldiers put pontoons across the river but made no effort to cross, *Lee* knew that this was a feint, and the main attack would be elsewhere. Cavalry reports of a large movement westward meant he should shift his troops in that direction. *Lee* left *Jubal Early* at Fredericksburg with 10,000 men and took 50,000 troops with him.

On May 1, 1863, advanced units of the armies clashed, and Hooker pulled back his army and began building defenses. After *Jeb Stuart's* cavalry reported that Hooker's right flank was "in the air" (unsupported), *Lee* and *Jackson* sat down on cracker boxes and drew up plans for a bold attack. *Jackson* was to take 26,000 men and move in front of the Union line around to its right flank. He would be aided by the thick undergrowth, but if he were attacked while on the move, or if *Lee's* 17,000 men were hit by Hooker's army, it would become a Confederate disaster.

Hooker's pickets observed *Jackson's* men on the road, but he paid no attention to the reports. At 6 p.m. on May 2, *Jackson* struck the west end of the Union line, driving the Yankees back in great confusion. That night, *Jackson* went out to observe the enemy positions in preparation for a night attack. One of his men, mistaking him for a Union solder, fired and wounded him. *Jackson* would die from the wound. *Stuart* took command of *Jackson's* men and continued the attack. Hooker still had numbers and the split in CSA forces as advantages, but the only aggressive action he took was to send Sedgwick against *Early*. After *Early* was pushed back, *Lee's* army went to support him and drove Sedgwick back. Hooker withdrew across the river, another humiliation for the "finest army on the planet" and for Lincoln.

Name _____

Class _____

POINTS TO CONSIDER

1. Hooker had often criticized Burnside. Do you feel that affected the way other officers felt about Hooker? Why?

_____

_____

_____

_____

_____

2. Lee's army was in much worse shape when it came to food and clothing than Hooker's. Explain why they felt so much better than did the men in the Army of the Potomac.

_____

_____

_____

_____

_____

3. Compare the qualities of Lee and Hooker that they demonstrated at Chancellorsville.

_____

_____

_____

_____

_____

Name _____

Class _____

CHALLENGES

1. What was Hooker's nickname?

_____

2. What problem did Lincoln see with his army?

_____

3. What did Hooker call his army?

_____

4. Whom did Hooker put in charge at Fredericksburg?

_____

5. Who discovered that Hooker's flank was "in the air"?

_____

6. How many of Lee's 43,000 men were taken for the attack on the flank?

_____

7. Why did that make Lee's situation more vulnerable?

_____

8. How was Jackson shot?

_____

9. What happened to Jackson as a result of the wound?

_____

10. What happened after Sedgwick took Fredericksburg?

_____

_____

VICKSBURG: THE ROCK THAT FINALLY FELL

Courtesy Library of Congress
John Pemberton

Vicksburg sat comfortably on a high bluff overlooking the Mississippi River and the marshy lowlands to the west. With 10 miles of defenses to its north and 40 miles to its south, Vicksburg's guns controlled the river, which made a large U-shaped bend just before it passed the guns guarding the city. After other river cities had fallen, only Vicksburg connected Texas, Arkansas, and Louisiana with the rest of the Confederacy. Two 1862 naval efforts by David Farragut against this "Gibralter" had failed. Grant wanted to try, and Halleck gave in: "Fight the enemy where you please."

Grant's efforts got off to a poor start. His first move was in December 1862. He led a 40,000-man army southward down the Mississippi Central Railroad, and Sherman, with 32,000 men, moved by boat down the river. Grant was thwarted when *Earl Van Dorn's* cavalry hit his main supply base at Holly Springs, Mississippi, and *Nathan B. Forrest's* cavalry tore up 60 miles of track behind him in Tennessee. Grant had to withdraw, but could not get word to Sherman, whose army was soon beaten back at Chickasaw Bluffs.

Grant made several attempts during the winter of 1863 to find a way to bypass the guns of Vicksburg. Nothing worked. Although Grant had little hope the projects would succeed, he thought it was better for his men to be working than loafing and getting soft.

In March 1863, Grant moved south by land on the west side of the river to a point below Vicksburg. David Porter, now in charge of the river fleet, was to run the guns of Vicksburg, and after reaching Grant's troops, ferry them across the river. Porter's fleet was spotted and shore guns blasted away; all 11 boats were hit, but only one was sunk. Porter's second fleet was not as lucky; it lost six barges and a transport.

To keep *John Pemberton,* the CSA commander at Vicksburg, from bothering his crossing, Grant had two diversions planned. Sherman's troops moved toward Chickasaw Bluffs, and Ben Grierson's cavalry hit a railroad used to supply Vicksburg from the east. His troops across the river, Grant headed toward the state capital of Jackson. After defeating *Johnston* there, Grant moved westward straight toward Vicksburg. CSA defenses were well prepared, and after attempts failed to break through them, Grant was forced to use a siege.

In the long siege, soldiers of the two armies became acquainted with each other. They traded bread for tobacco one day, and the next, tried to kill each other.

Conditions inside the city became primitive. Shellings made it unsafe to live in houses, so the citizens dug caves in the bluffs. Food was very short, and they ate horses, mules, dogs, cats, and muskrats. It was agreed inside Vicksburg that the food supply was dangerously low. If the Yankees made a strong charge, the defenses could fail. *Pemberton* arranged with Grant for his troops to be paroled, rather than sent to a prison camp.

The date of the surrender was July 4, 1863. Grant captured 31,600 soldiers, 172 cannons, 60,000 muskets, and a large supply of ammunition. But as great as his achievement was, the nations' eyes were focused on Gettysburg that day.

Name _____

Class _____

POINTS TO CONSIDER

1. Why was the role of the navy so important to Grant's success?

_____

_____

_____

_____

_____

2. During the winter of 1863, northern newspapers were demanding that Grant be fired because his projects of digging canals failed. Why do you think Lincoln resisted the urge to do the popular thing and fire him?

_____

_____

_____

_____

3. Many troops at Vicksburg and residents of the city were furious with Pemberton for surrendering on Independence Day. Why?

_____

_____

_____

_____

Name _____

Class _____

CHALLENGES

1. How many total miles around Vicksburg were fortified?

_____

2. What naval officer had failed in two attempts at Vicksburg in 1862?

_____

3. Who messed up Grant's attack in December 1862?

_____

4. What battle did Sherman fight and lose?

_____

5. Why did Grant try projects in the winter of 1863 that he did not expect to succeed?

_____

6. What Union cavalry officer made a famous raid that took attention off of Grant?

_____

7. Whom did Grant defeat at Jackson?

_____

8. What were people forced to eat during the siege of Vicksburg?

_____

9. What reasons did Pemberton have to surrender the city?

_____

_____

10. How many CSA troops were surrendered at Vicksburg?

_____

GETTYSBURG: THE ACCIDENTAL BATTLE

Gettysburg, July 1863

The victorious Army of Northern Virginia had demonstrated its skill at Chancellorsville, and its spirit couldn't have been higher. Western CSA armies were in trouble, however. Grant had moved south of Vicksburg, captured Jackson, and was closing in on Vicksburg from the east. *Longstreet* wanted to go to Tennessee and help *Braxton Bragg* in the Chattanooga area, but *Lee* had a different plan: invade Pennsylvania. This could accomplish several things: encourage Peace Democrats, force Federal troops in Tennessee and Mississippi to be pulled east, and allow his army to live off food and supplies taken from the Yankees for a change.

After *Jackson's* death, *Lee* reorganized his army into three corps instead of two. Commanders were now *Longstreet, Richard Ewell,* and *A.P. Hill.* When the army moved, it was important that Hooker not know where they were or where they were going. Hooker guessed they were moving, and his cavalry met *Stuart's* in the Battle of Brandy Station—the largest cavalry battle of the war. For the first time, Union cavalry performed as well as Rebel, and *Stuart* received much public criticism. More important, Hooker now knew where *Lee* was. *Ewell* had a much easier time than *Stuart* in defeating Robert Milroy at Winchester.

By mid-June, the Rebels were in Pennsylvania, visiting farmers, merchants, and stores, paying for what they took in Confederate money. On June 23, *Stuart's* cavalry headed east to harrass the Yankees, destroy their supplies, and gather information. *Stuart's* instructions were vague, but his trip took far too long, and *Lee* lost the "eyes of his army." *Lee's* army spread over a large area 100 miles west to east and 40 miles north to south. Hooker suggested to Lincoln that this was an ideal time to attack Richmond; the president told him that *Lee's* army was more important to defeat than seizing the Confederate capital. Lincoln had lost confidence in Hooker and decided it was time to change commanders.

The responsibility of stopping *Lee's* advance fell to George Meade. Unlike Hooker, who wanted to lead the Army of the Potomac, Meade was content to let someone else lead, but on June 28, 1863, Meade was told to assume command. Meade was an able officer, but his hot temper made him unpopular, and his troops described him as a "goggle-eyed snapping turtle."

Lee hoped to avoid any major battle until his army was reunited, so when he learned on June 28 that the Yankees were north of the Potomac, he sent an order for all units to gather near Gettysburg. *A.P. Hill,* already near Gettysburg, decided to visit the town and take the shoes that were reported to have been stored there. Arriving on July 1, he found that John Buford's cavalry was already there. Then John Reynolds arrived, and soon *Ewell* was there to support *Hill.* Over the next three days, one of the world's most important battles took place as both sides fought for the hills near this quiet town.

Name _____

Class_____

POINTS TO CONSIDER

1. If you had been on Lee's staff, would you have argued for or against the march into Pennsylvania? Why?

_____

_____

_____

_____

_____

2. When Lee's troops bought eggs from farmers and paid for them with Confederate money, do you think the Pennsylvania farmers were satisfied with the deal? Why?

_____

_____

_____

_____

3. If you had been in Meade's army, would you have been more enthused about fighting in Pennsylvania than you had been in Virginia? Explain.

_____

_____

_____

_____

Name _____

Class _____

CHALLENGES

1. What did Longstreet want to do to help armies in the West?

_____

2. How did Lee want to help them?

_____

3. Who was in command of Federal forces when Lee moved out in June?

_____

4. What large cavalry battle was fought?

_____

5. As they entered Pennsylvania, what job was Stuart assigned?

_____

6. How did Hooker want to handle the Rebel invasion?

_____

7. What did Lincoln think was the job of the Army of the Potomac?

_____

8. Who replaced Hooker?

_____

9. Why was A.P. Hill interested in going to Gettysburg?

_____

10. What Federal general arrived to support Buford?

_____

What CSA general arrived to support Hill?

_____

GETTYSBURG: SHOWDOWN AT CEMETERY RIDGE

Gateway of Gettysburg Cemetery, July 1863

While no one had selected Gettysburg as the place to fight the battle of the century, once there, *Lee* decided that Meade must be engaged there. *Longstreet* did not like the strength of Union positions south of town, but *Lee* saw the only options as fight or retreat. When he requested that *Ewell* press the enemy "if possible" on the late afternoon of July 1, *Ewell* did not attack. With *Stuart's* cavalry away, *Lee* had no idea of the huge army being assembled by the Yankees. When Meade arrived on July 2, he found his army numbered 93,000 and controlled the ridges.

Meade's first concern was protecting the Baltimore Pike, which could be used by the Confederates to attack Washington. However, action shifted to the west side of Cemetery Hill and Cemetery Ridge after *Longstreet* tried to flank the Union left. Acting on his own, Dan Sickles moved his troops on Cemetery Ridge, leaving a gap in the line between any Federal troops and Little Round Top. Gouverneur Warren saw the gap and rushed troops to this key point, arriving barely ahead of the Rebels, whom his troops managed to beat off. *Longstreet* then shifted his attack to Sickles, whose men were pushed back through the Peach Orchard, Wheat Field, and Devil's Den. It was all in vain, however, as Federal reserves managed to hold them back.

Lee's army had suffered heavy losses, but had also inflicted them. He felt that with one grand rush, he might be able to break the Federals' spirit. That task was assigned to the troops of *George Pickett. Longstreet* was strongly opposed to this move, but gave up when he saw *Lee* had made up his mind. The first gun duel of July 3 was on the eastern flank of the line, where *Ewell's* troops were driven off Culp's Hill. Then there was a stillness in the hot air, as each army prepared for the coming storm.

It struck at 1:00 as 140 Confederate cannons opened fire and 118 Federal cannons responded. The artillery went at each other for two hours. When *Porter Alexander*, in charge of artillery, informed *Longstreet* that he was running short on ammunition, it was time for *Pickett* to move. His 10,500 men formed in three ranks as if on parade, and at 3:10 p.m., they moved forward at 110 paces a minute. The Federals fired everything available at them, but the gray wave kept coming, and some reached the Yankee line before being killed or captured. It had been a heroic effort, but a dismal failure. As the survivors returned, *Lee* met them and tried to encourage them. When *Pickett* saw *Lee*, he was told to move his division behind the woods; *Pickett* replied: "General Lee, I have no division."

Lee, Longstreet, and others in the high command prepared for Meade to attack their weakened troops, but Meade felt his men were too tired. On July 4, the Confederates began to withdraw, but heavy rains prevented recrossing the Potomac until July 13. Lincoln was very disappointed in Meade's lack of movement after the battle. Casualties on both sides totalled at least 47,000 men.

109   *Southern military leaders are in italics.

Name _____

Class _____

POINTS TO CONSIDER

1. What do you think caused Lee to overestimate what his army could do and underestimate the Federal army?

_____

_____

_____

_____

_____

2. You were a soldier in Pickett's Charge. What would you be thinking as you formed your line?

_____

_____

_____

_____

_____

3. The fact that the Army of Northern Virginia had escaped left many in the North wondering at the casualties caused by the war. That was the reason why Lincoln felt he should go to the dedication of the cemetery there and give a short speech. After reading the Gettysburg Address, try to paraphrase it (put it in your own words).

_____

_____

_____

_____

Name _____

Class _____

CHALLENGES

1. Why did Lee decide to fight at Gettysburg?

_____

_____

2. Why was Meade first concerned about the Baltimore Pike?

_____

3. What area of the battlefield did Sickles leave open?

_____

4. What did Lee want to accomplish with Pickett's Charge?

_____

_____

5. Who was opposed to the idea?

_____

6. What happened to Ewell's troops on the morning of July 3?

_____

_____

7. In the duel between cannons, how many guns were involved?

_____

8. How many men were involved in Pickett's Charge?

_____

9. Why did Meade not attack on July 4?

_____

10. Was Lincoln pleased with Meade after Lee crossed the Potomac?

_____

THE UNION HIGH COMMAND: GRANT IN CHARGE

Courtesy Peter A. Juley & Son

Ulysses S. Grant

By 1864, many Union generals important in the beginning of the war were gone; they had failed to win battles and now were either out of the army or left in less important roles. Irvin McDowell, who lost at Bull Run, now led the Army of the Pacific. George McClellan went home after Antietam to wait for new orders; he never received them. John Pope, loser at Second Bull Run, was sent to work out problems with the Sioux Indians. Ambrose Burnside, defeated at Fredericksburg, was now working under Grant. Joe Hooker, after Chancellorsville, served in battles like Chickamauga, Chattanooga, and Lookout Mountain. No matter how well he did, Hooker never received the credit from Grant that was given to Sherman.

The man chosen by the Constitution as commander in chief was Lincoln. No other president faced the problems he did in raising and supplying an army anywhere near the size of the Union army. No president had ever dealt with such complex military strategy questions. A president needs good help in such times. His first secretary of war, Simon Cameron, never got a handle on his job, but his second man, Edwin Stanton, brought some order to it. The quartermaster general, Montgomery Meigs, did an excellent job of supplying the troops with clothing, shoes, and food. No army had ever eaten as well. Many mistakes were made at first, but Lincoln learned quickly. In this, he had help from General Henry Halleck, whose main talent was explaining military problems and strategies to civilians.

When Ulysses Grant was named general in chief, it was a title well deserved. However, his friend Sherman warned him against the political intrigue around Washington and advised that he set up headquarters elsewhere. The eastern soldiers were prepared to hate him, but Grant was so unassuming that he changed many of their minds. One officer saw only three emotions in him: "deep thought, extreme determination, and great simplicity and calmness." Critics were also there, pointing out his reputation for drinking, his poor grammar, and his inability to march in step.

Like Grant, William T. Sherman had been unsuccessful in civilian life, but war had changed him. When it began, he wanted to play it by the old rules: no stealing, robbery, or pillage. By 1864, he wrote Halleck: "We are not only fighting hostile armies, but a hostile people, and must make old and young, rich and poor, feel the hard hand of war." With the war nearly won, the "better angel of his nature" returned, and he became more benevolent.

Other generals in the Federal army provided a wide variety of skills and personalities. If one preferred the colorful, George Custer was the man. Last in his class at West Point in 1861, he was a major general, U.S. Volunteers, in 1865. Ben Butler was controversial but protected from being punished for his mistakes because he was a Democrat, and Lincoln needed support for the war from the opposition party.

Serving in this army was a future road to the presidency. In addition to Grant, Rutherford B. Hayes, James Garfield, Chester Arthur, and Benjamin Harrison were generals; William McKinley was a major.

Name _____

Class _____

POINTS TO CONSIDER

1. Make a list of things that Lincoln had to learn more about as a wartime president that he might have known little about when he took the job.

_____

_____

_____

_____

_____

2. Grant and Sherman both failed as civilians. Do you think that helped or hurt them as generals? Why?

_____

_____

_____

_____

_____

3. What qualities do you think a good general would have to have in a war?

_____

_____

_____

_____

_____

Name _____

Class _____

CHALLENGES

1. What did McDowell and Pope have in common in 1864?

_____

2. What two former commanders where now working for Grant?

_____

3. What is the job of quartermaster general?

_____

4. Who had the job of explaining military tactics to Lincoln?

_____

5. What good characteristics were noted about Grant?

_____

_____

6. What did Grant's critics object to?

_____

_____

7. What was Halleck's chief contribution?

_____

8. In the early days of the war, what was Sherman's attitude toward involving civilians?

_____

_____

9. Who was the most colorful Federal general?

_____

10. How many generals went on to become president after the war?

_____

FROM THE WILDERNESS TO COLD HARBOR

Extreme Line of Confederate Works, Cold Harbor

Ulysses Grant was a survivor. He was forced to resign from the army in 1854, reentered the army in 1861 only through political pull, and even with his record of victories, he had twice been relieved of command. In spite of Grant's critics, President Lincoln admired him as a fighter who did his best with whatever he had. After lifting the siege at Chattanooga, Grant was called to Washington, where Lincoln promoted him to lieutenant general in the Regular Army and gave him the responsibility of designing all Union strategy. Grant was an active man who preferred a saddle to a desk. He would go with the Army of the Potomac as it moved against *Lee*. He promised Lincoln that no matter what happened, he would not turn back.

On May 4, 1864, Grant's army crossed the Rapidan River and moved into that region of Virginia known as the Wilderness. The location suited *Lee* better than Grant. Its dense woods cancelled the Union's advantage in cavalry and artillery. One soldier described the battle as one without a front or a rear, and another said they were two "howling mobs." Each army had its opportunity to win a major victory. Winfield Hancock's troops broke the CSA line on May 6, but just as they came to the clearing where *Lee's* headquarters was, *Longstreet's* fresh troops arrived and drove them back. Later that same day, *Longstreet* broke Hancock's flank, but was shot by one of his own men as he rode back from the line. Brush fires broke out, and at times the battle stopped so the wounded could be rescued. Grant was told what *Lee* would probably do next; he told his officers not to think about *Lee*, but "try to think what we are going to do for ourselves."

On May 7, the armies rested and waited for orders. That evening, the word came from Grant: the Union army was heading south to Spotsylvania. This move was no surprise to *Lee*, who reasoned that if he were Grant, that would be his target. *Richard Anderson* (now commanding *Longstreet's* men) had dug five miles of trenches before the Yankees arrived. Shaped like the letter U, the trenches allowed CSA troops to easily move from one position to another and meet Union advances head on. Colonel Emory Upton broke through the line, but was driven back. Then Hancock got through; *Lee* was there at the front, but his soldiers shouted "General Lee to the rear" and drove Hancock's men back. The weakest spot in the U became known as "Bloody Angle" because of the fierce fighting there. The dead lay three deep in the muddy trenches at Bloody Angle. In less than three weeks, the Union had lost 6,300 soldiers, but Grant relentlessly moved toward Cold Harbor.

General Phil Sheridan's cavalry beat *Lee* in the race this time, but the Rebel infantry was soon in position and digging in. As Union soldiers prepared to attack the Confederate line, they pinned pieces of paper with their names on them to their uniforms, so their families would know where they died. The attack on June 3 was costly for Grant's army, as the men in gray blasted them with rifle and cannon.

Name _____

Class _____

POINTS TO CONSIDER

1. As a veteran soldier in Grant's army, how does your new general seem different to you than those of the past?

_____

_____

_____

_____

_____

2. What do you think it would have been like to fight at the Bloody Angle?

_____

_____

_____

_____

3. If you were Lincoln, what kinds of political problems would Grant be causing for you in May and June, 1864?

_____

_____

_____

_____

Name _____

Class _____

CHALLENGES

1. What rank was Grant given in 1864?

_____

2. What assignment did Lincoln give him?

_____

3. What did Grant promise to Lincoln?

_____

4. Why did the Wilderness suit Lee better than Grant?

_____

_____

5. What CSA general was wounded at the Battle of the Wilderness?

_____

6. Why was fighting interrupted during the battle?

_____

7. Name two Union officers successful (for a while) at Spotsylvania.

_____

8. Where did the worst fighting at Spotsylvania take place?

_____

9. Why did soldiers pin their names on their uniforms at Cold Harbor?

_____

_____

10. What happened when Grant attacked June 3?

_____

SHERMAN TAKES ATLANTA AND MARCHES THROUGH GEORGIA

William T. Sherman

When Grant took command of the army, he entrusted the command of his western army to William T. Sherman. Like Grant, "Cump" Sherman had been a failure for most of his civilian life, but then the Civil War came. At first, he had many critics who pointed out his exaggeration of southern forces in Kentucky and who claimed he was insane. He and Grant first teamed up in the battles at Ft. Henry and Ft. Donelson and became close friends.

With Grant promoted to general in chief and going east to take charge of the campaign against *Lee,* he could no longer actively lead the army in the West, so he entrusted that job to Sherman. While Grant pressed *Lee's* army, Sherman was to drive toward Atlanta, and once it was taken, to march toward the Atlantic coast. General *Joe Johnston* intended to block him. Knowing Sherman had the advantage of numbers, *Johnston's* plan was to find a good position, dig in, make the enemy pay a terrible price for the trench, and when the time came, drop back to another good defensive position. With high enough casualties, the Democrats would win the 1864 election and make peace. His army was ragged and hungry, but they were very loyal to him. Slowly withdrawing, *Johnston* gave up Dalton, Resaca, Cassville, and Kennesaw Mountain. Grant and Sherman respected his ability, but President Davis did not like him or his strategy. After Generals *Braxton Bragg* and *John Hood* falsely accused *Johnston* of having no plans for the defense of Atlanta, Davis relieved *Johnston* of command on July 17, 1864, and appointed *Hood* as his replacement.

Hood was described by *Lee* as "all lion and no fox." His courage was unquestioned. His arm was crippled at Gettysburg, a leg was amputated after Chickamauga, and he had to be strapped in his saddle to ride. The army was furious at the change of command, and even *Hood* became uncertain that he was the right choice. By this time, the Confederates were backed up to the 12 miles of trenches protecting Atlanta. Rather than wait for Sherman to attack, *Hood* sent armies out to strike him first, but they were repulsed at Peachtree Creek. *William Hardee* then tried to break the Union line east of the city, but that move also failed. Sherman, however, was also having trouble. *S.D. Lee* held off a Union advance at Ezra's Church, west of Atlanta, and *Joe Wheeler's* cavalry defeated three larger Union cavalry units.

Sherman began shelling Atlanta while sending his troops in a wide arc to cut off its railroad connections to the south. Failing to drive off Union troops at Jonesboro, *Hood* set fire to everything of military value and left Atlanta on September 1, 1864. Sherman telegraphed Lincoln that "Atlanta is ours, and fairly won." Sherman ordered everyone to leave the city, then in November he burned the city, and his army began its famous March to the Sea. *Hood* moved northward, but General George Thomas, with 60,000 men, kept him from doing much harm. For Sherman's 62,000 men, the March to the Sea was almost a peaceful stroll. On December 21, 1864, Savannah fell.

118 *Southern military leaders are in italics.

Name _____

Class _____

POINTS TO CONSIDER

1. Johnston's tactics kept losing territory to the Union army. Do you think President Davis was right in removing him?

_____

_____

_____

_____

_____

2. As a CSA soldier, what would you think when you saw Hood ride in to take command?

_____

_____

_____

_____

3. Sherman believed in "total war:" fighting armies and destroying cities, towns, and farms along the way. Do you go along with this idea, or do you feel civilians should not be the target of armies?

_____

_____

_____

_____

_____

Name _____

Class _____

CHALLENGES

1. Where did Sherman and Grant start working together?

_____

2. What made it possible for Sherman to assume command in the West?

_____

3. What was the city he was ordered to capture?

_____

4. Who was the first CSA commander to oppose him?

_____

5. What major battles were fought as the Confederates retreated?

_____

6. Who persuaded President Davis to fire Johnston?

_____

7. How did Hood try to defend Atlanta?

_____

_____

8. What Confederate cavalry officer did an outstanding job?

_____

9. Why was Sherman unpopular among Atlantans for many years after the war?

_____

10. What was the first seacoast city to fall to Sherman?

_____

LET US HAVE PEACE, NOW!

Horace Greeley

This was supposed to be a short war, so many people had said. The longer it lasted, the less patient many were with Lincoln, Davis, the fumbling generals, the awful sights and smells of the battlefield, and the sad but frequent experience of attending memorial services for brave men.

Many northern Democrats blamed the war on the Republicans. If Lincoln had not been elected, there might not have been a war. Some did not like blacks and feared that when the war was over, thousands of freed blacks would rush north and take their jobs away from them. Critics accused Lincoln of abusing his power by taking away *habeas corpus,* or they were workers hurt by the loss of trade with the South. Their enthusiasm for peace at any price caused others to suspect they were allies of the South (and some were). Republicans found a name for them—Copperheads.

The Knights of the Golden Circle (KGC) had been formed in the 1850s, but was given new life by the war. It was one of many Copperhead groups. Rumors spread throughout the North of a conspiracy by the KGC to overthrow the government. The KGC had only a few members, but rumors made it seem like a major threat. The Order of American Knights (OAK) formed in 1863 and urged men to avoid the draft. Copperhead leaders met with southern agents and wanted to use the Democratic convention in 1864 as a time to have an uprising in the North against Lincoln and the war. After a few ringleaders were arrested, the plot failed.

When Democrats won 9 of the 14 Illinois House seats in 1862, Corporal Adolphus Wolf wrote home: "Tell Father to buy a good revolver [to defend himself from the Copperheads]. It would be a blessing to the country, to clear it of all such vile traitors."

The "Heroes of America" were the South's version of the Copperheads. They too had secret passwords and rituals. The group was supported by the editor of the important Raleigh *North Carolina Standard;* its editor wanted North Carolina to secede from the Confederacy. Even in Mississippi, President Davis's home state, peace agitation was strong, and by 1864, many there wanted to return to the Union.

Private individuals who wanted peace tried to find terms that would end the war. In 1864, Thomas Yeatman from Tennessee met with Ambassador Charles Francis Adams in England. He told Adams that Davis would step down as Confederate president if Lincoln would agree to pay owners for slaves that were freed. The only problem was that Yeatman had no authority to make a deal. Horace Greeley, editor of the New York *Tribune* heard from a man named Jewett, who said CSA agents who were in Canada had power to make peace. Greeley met them, but found they had no power and were only trying to stir up anti-Lincoln agitation. These and other efforts were doomed to fail. The South demanded independence, and Lincoln was not about to let them have it.

Name _____

Class _____

POINTS TO CONSIDER

1. Do you think Copperheads were more interested in attacking Lincoln than they were in making peace?

_____

_____

_____

_____

_____

2. Think of reasons that might explain Adolphus Wolf's attitude toward Copperheads. Do you think he was justified in feeling that way? Why or why not?

_____

_____

_____

_____

_____

3. Do you think that when it came to peace movements, both Lincoln and Davis faced very similar problems?

_____

_____

_____

_____

_____

Name _____

Class _____

CHALLENGES

1. Democrats blamed Lincoln for the war. What was their argument?

_____

_____

2. What nickname did the Republicans give peace Democrats?

_____

3. Which group was rumored to have been plotting to overthrow the U.S. government?

_____

4. Was there any truth to rumors that Democrats were secretly meeting with southern agents?

_____

5. What was Corporal Wolf's opinion of Copperheads?

_____

_____

6. What was the southern version of Copperheads?

_____

7. What Confederate newspaper supported the peace movement?

_____

8. Who met with Ambassador Adams to talk about peace?

_____

_____

9. Why did the talks fail?

_____

_____

10. What northern newspaper editor tried without success to make peace?

_____

THE LINCOLN CABINET: INTERNAL CIVIL WAR

William Seward

If you had asked the average Republican in early 1860 who was the most important member of the party, the answer you would have most likely heard was William Seward or Salmon Chase, not Lincoln. Only six years old, the Republican party had brought together an odd collection of members: Whigs, unhappy Democrats, Free Soilers, and reformers interested in many different causes. No one person could claim that he invented the Republican party. Many leaders were old rivals and political enemies.

William Seward took the secretary of state job because he thought it would make him the real power in government. A former governor and senator, he often made statements that caused problems for himself later. Strongly anti-slavery, he said in 1850 there was a "higher law than the Constitution" and talked about an "irrepressible conflict" in an 1858 speech. He made Lincoln wonder about his new secretary of state when he suggested the U.S. make war on France and Spain and "wrap the world in flames." After a mild rebuke by Lincoln, he quieted down and did an effective job.

The secretary of the treasury was Salmon Chase, who as Ohio's attorney general had defended many fugitive slaves. He had gone on to become governor and senator. Like Seward, he thought he should have been the Republican presidential candidate and made no secret of his opinion that he was smarter than Lincoln. Self-righteous and without humor, he and Lincoln were much different in approach to issues and people.

Edwin Stanton became secretary of war in 1862. Stanton was a Democrat, had backed Breckinridge in 1860, and had criticized Lincoln; yet Lincoln chose him for his Cabinet. Stanton was very efficient and soon had the War Department operating smoothly. He was not easy to like, however.

Washington is a city that thrives on rumors, and during the Civil War there were more than usual. A common one was that Lincoln was under Seward's thumb—that Seward was the "evil genius" in the administration. Lincoln and Seward knew better, but Chase believed it and talked with his Radical Republican friends about it. After the disaster at Fredericksburg, criticism of Lincoln was common, and rumors spread that the Cabinet—and maybe even Lincoln—were going to resign.

Seward turned in his resignation, in order to relieve pressure on Lincoln, but no one else knew that. A group of senators came to see Lincoln and blamed Seward for being lukewarm in the conduct of the war. The president said little, but invited the senators to return the next day. When they came, they found all the Cabinet except Seward present, and Lincoln told them the Cabinet was always consulted, but he made all the decisions. Then Lincoln asked the Cabinet to confirm what he had said. Chase made a brief statement agreeing with the president. The next day, Chase offered to resign. Lincoln then turned down both resignations, and the Cabinet was not changed. One thing had been accomplished: Chase and Seward had both learned a valuable lesson in politics from Lincoln.

Name _____

Class _____

POINTS TO CONSIDER

1. What would have happened if Lincoln had fired Chase?

_____

_____

_____

_____

2. What would have happened if Lincoln accepted Seward's resignation?

_____

_____

_____

_____

3. How would you have felt if you had been Seward or Chase and the president turned down your letter of resignation?

_____

_____

_____

_____

Name _____

Class _____

CHALLENGES

1. Where was Seward from?

_____

2. What important offices had he held before becoming secretary of state?

_____

3. How had he gotten himself into controversy before?

_____

4. What important offices had Chase held?

_____

5. Why was Chase hard to get along with?

_____

6. According to rumors, which one dominated Lincoln?

_____

7. What party did Stanton belong to?

_____

8. What battle caused great criticism of Lincoln's Cabinet?

_____

9. What accusation did the senators make against Seward?

_____

_____

10. Why did Lincoln arrange the second meeting with the senators?

_____

_____

THE ELECTION OF 1864: LINCOLN vs. McCLELLAN

Courtesy New-York Historical Society
George McClellan

The Constitution requires that the presidential election be held every four years, but in most countries, a civil war would justify to an unpopular leader that circumstances require that he call off the election. No one in either party suggested that the election be delayed.

Lincoln was far from confident as the Republican convention approached in 1864. Too many battles had been lost: Bull Run, Seven Days, Second Bull Run, Fredericksburg, and Chancellorsville among them. Victories had been hard won at Antietam, Vicksburg, and Gettysburg. Brighter days might be ahead, but would voters forget disasters of the past?

Critics seemed almost everywhere. Senator Ben Wade bluntly told Lincoln: "You are the father of every military blunder that has been made during the war. This government is on the road to Hell." Others preferred to criticize him behind his back. Senator Samuel Pomeroy of Kansas issued the Pomeroy Circular, which was to be a "strictly private" letter urging that Lincoln be dropped from the ticket and Chase replace him. Chase was embarrassed and offered to resign (again), but Lincoln refused (again). Another group wanted General John C. Frémont, but so many Democrats were in that movement that no important Republican supported Frémont.

Meeting in Baltimore, the Republicans (who now called themselves the National Union party) chose Lincoln for a second term, with Democrat Andrew Johnson for vice president. Lincoln said that the party had decided it was best not to "swap horses while crossing the river." Horace Greeley was among those who believed the party was doomed with Lincoln as the candidate, and he and others supported Frémont's Radical Democracy ticket. Fremont's group folded later and supported Lincoln.

The Democratic convention was held in Chicago, and its delegates were split between supporters and opponents of the war. The platform adopted called for both continuing the war and for peace. The candidate chosen was George B. McClellan, the twice-removed general. McClellan tried to separate himself from the Peace Democrats, but Republicans would not let the Democratic platform die as an issue.

Lincoln needed help to win, and his generals cooperated. Sheridan's campaign in the Shenandoah Valley was so successful that James Garfield called it "a speech . . . more powerful and valuable to the Union cause than all the stumpers in the Republic." General Custer displayed captured enemy battle flags in Washington. But even more useful were the 10,000 soldiers sent home by Sheridan to vote in the presidential election. Of soldiers who cast absentee votes, three out of four voted for Lincoln.

In electoral votes, Lincoln won 212-12. McClellan carried only three states. In the House, Republicans outnumbered Democrats 145-40, and in the Senate, the margin was 41-10.

Lincoln's second inaugural (March 4, 1865) was directed at healing the wounds left by the war, "to care for him who shall have borne the battle and for his widow and orphan, to do all which may achieve and cherish a just and lasting peace among ourselves and with all nations."

Name _____

Class _____

POINTS TO CONSIDER

1. You are President Lincoln in 1864, and you worry that you will lose the election. What kinds of excuses could you come up with for calling it off?

_____

_____

_____

_____

2. While Lincoln had a hard time during this campaign, so did McClellan. If you were running the McClellan campaign, what kinds of problems would you have?

_____

_____

_____

_____

3. Lincoln's second inaugural began to focus on the future. If Lincoln had lived, what kinds of issues would he have faced after the war?

_____

_____

_____

_____

CHALLENGES

1. Name two Senate critics of Lincoln.

_____

2. Who did Pomeroy favor as the presidential candidate?

_____

3. What former presidential candidate also received some support?

_____

4. What policies did the Democratic platform call for in 1864?

_____

5. Who was the Democratic candidate in 1864?

_____

6. In what two ways did Sheridan help Lincoln?

_____

_____

7. How did Custer help Lincoln?

_____

_____

8. How many more electoral votes did Lincoln have than McClellan?

_____

9. How many more Republicans were in the House than Democrats?

_____

10. How many more Republicans were in the Senate than Democrats?

_____

CIVILIAN LIFE IN THE NORTH DURING THE WAR

Tom Thumb and Lavinia Warren

If wars are hard on some, others benefit from new opportunities. The manufacturer, railroad owner, the worker drawing higher wages, and the person who has special talents may all profit from the war.

Individuals who became famous later were going into business at the time of the Civil War. Gail Borden began producing condensed milk. John D. Rockefeller bought his first oil refinery. Jay Cooke opened his banking house in 1861 and made a fortune selling U.S. and state bonds during the war. Those providing the army with uniforms, tents, shoes, saddles, and a wide variety of other items made fortunes, especially the dishonest ones. Then there were the greedy in the army, like Andrew Butler (brother of General Ben Butler), who sold Confederate cotton and pocketed the money.

A good example of how some people thought occurred in 1864 when Joseph Howard, editor of the Brooklyn *Eagle,* plotted to make a fortune in the gold market. He inserted a phony article in New York newspapers saying that Lincoln had asked for a national day of "fasting, humiliation, and prayer." He was caught and jailed for three months. A more common get-rich-quick scheme was to gamble in greenbacks, buying them after defeats, selling them at great profit after victories. Small time operators took bounties for joining the army, then deserted many times.

But there were honest ways to make money as well. Farm products had a large market, not only selling to the army and northern civilians, but to England and Europe, where drought had caused crop failures. This was at the same time thousands of farmers were being drafted. New farm equipment was needed to produce more with less help; in 1862, 490 patents were issued for new farm machinery. Those who made steam boilers for the navy and merchant ships had more customers than ever before.

Average citizens did not do these things, but spent their days working on the farm or in the shop. Wages went up during the war, but barely kept up with the higher costs of everything else. There were changes in the work force. More women were working, many in government agencies, sewing uniforms for soldiers, or plowing fields. Blacks were also looking for jobs, but few found jobs that paid well. When a union struck, employers often used black strikebreakers. This made them unpopular with union members and added to tension between poor whites and blacks.

War news occupied people's thoughts. The leading newspaper of the time was Horace Greeley's New York *Tribune. Harper's Weekly* magazine not only told war news, but its artists let the public see where battles were being fought. Matthew Brady's photographs of battlefields left no doubt that the war was real. The public looked for other, less serious events to think about, and P.T. Barnum supplied one. His star performer, 27-inch Tom Thumb, married 24-inch Lavinia Warren in a ceremony attended by generals, governors, and members of Congress.

Name_____

Class_____

POINTS TO CONSIDER

1. Why do wars make it possible for greedy people to make fortunes?

_____

_____

_____

_____

_____

2. How did farmers gain from the war?

_____

_____

_____

_____

3. Why would an event like Tom Thumb's wedding draw so much attention when battles were being fought and great issues were being debated?

_____

_____

_____

_____

Name _____

Class _____

CHALLENGES

1. What business did Gail Borden enter?

_____

2. What business was John D. Rockefeller in?

_____

3. Who sold Confederate cotton and pocketed the money?

_____

4. What was Joseph Howard speculating in?

_____

5. As a person interested in becoming a greenback speculator, would you want the North to win or lose their next battle?

_____

6. Were farmers making more money during the war?

_____

7. Why were blacks unpopular with union members?

_____

_____

8. What was the leading northern newspaper in the 1860s?

_____

9. Who was its publisher?

_____

10. What couple got married during the war and attracted much attention?

_____

THE SOUTH DURING THE WAR: DOING WITHOUT

A Confederate bond used as money by the Confederate government during the Civil War.

The four years of war discouraged all but the most devoted Confederates. Faced with enormous prices for everything, a shopper went into the store with a wheelbarrow full of cash to buy a sackful of groceries. The soldier wondered if he should not desert and care for his starving family. Those who were in battle areas or were driven out of their homes by Yankee soldiers became refugees looking for a meal to eat and a place to lie down at night. The transportation system was being destroyed by Sherman's troops. Gangs of hoodlums, including deserters of both armies, picked on the helpless and, in some areas, simply took over.

There were shortages of almost everything. Food was in short supply, especially in cities where speculators held out for higher prices. This led to rioting and looting in Richmond. In April 1862, a mob attacked warehouses and smashed store windows grabbing jewelry and shoes. President Davis arrived and appealed to the mob to go home. He threw them some money and, to show it was all he had, he turned his pockets inside out. Then he pulled out his watch and told them that if they were not gone in five minutes, he would order the militia to fire on them. The crowd disappeared, but the food shortage only got worse.

Crime rose as law and order collapsed. By 1864, in some parts of the South, there were no sheriffs or police to arrest the criminals and no judges to hear their cases. Deserters gathered in the mountains, swamps, and remote areas and literally took over. In a few cases, the Confederate army was sent to round them up, but this took troops away from the war and did not solve the problem.

Money was at the root of both food and crime problems. Secretary of Treasury Christopher Memminger urged the Confederate Congress to pay for the war with taxes, but he was ignored. The CSA assumed that citizen loyalty would be weakened by heavy taxes. At first they were able to get around the money shortage by seizing federal assets. Then they tried borrowing. In 1862, Erlanger & Co. in Paris agreed to market Confederate bonds in return for a large commission for itself. At first the bonds sold well, but sales dropped quickly after Gettysburg and Vicksburg. All else failing, the CSA printed money at a rapid pace.

Refugees were chased from their homes either as the result of battles in the backyard or because Sherman or some other Union officer ordered them out. It is estimated that about 175,000-200,000 southerners were refugees for an extended period of time. Usually they drifted to cities or tried to find a family member who would take them in. Those most accepted were ministers, teachers, and physicians. The least wanted were proud aristocrats, the poor, and draft dodgers.

The South's enthusiasm for war was declining after the summer of 1863, and only grim determination to hold on was left in its place.

Name _____

Class _____

POINTS TO CONSIDER

1. How do you think crime was related to the money problem in the South?

_____

_____

_____

_____

_____

2. How do you think the army's high desertion rate at the end of the war was related to the money problem?

_____

_____

_____

_____

3. How did refugees make the situation worse for the rest of the South?

_____

_____

_____

_____

_____

Name _____

Class _____

CHALLENGES

1. Where did the most serious bread riot occur?

_____

2. Who successfully stopped it?

_____

3. Why did criminals have an easy time of it in some parts of the South?

_____

_____

4. What areas had the most crime?

_____

5. How did Secretary Memminger want to pay for the war?

_____

6. How did the Confederate Congress decide to pay for it?

_____

_____

7. What French company handled the largest sale of Confederate bonds?

_____

8. What caused Europeans to stop buying Confederate bonds?

_____

9. About how many refugees were driven from their homes for long periods of time?

_____

10. Which refugees were most welcome?

_____

PETERSBURG IS BESIEGED

Ft. Sedgwick, one of the earthwork fortifications in the Union line surrounding Petersburg.

The CSA was being taken apart, one big chunk after another. When Vicksburg fell in 1863, the western part of the Confederacy was sliced off from the east. Then Sherman's march to Atlanta was beginning to carve off Mississippi, Alabama, Florida, and southern Georgia. To the modern person with a map and calculator, it would seem the war was about over. The Union army could draft more men and build more guns, but the South was about out of able-bodied men, and its food and military resources were running low. The South was almost taking pride in its stubborn refusal to quit. If Lincoln were to lose the 1864 election, the CSA might yet be able to make peace with a more reasonable McClellan administration.

To describe what happened in an orderly way is almost impossible. Grant and *Lee* were both trying to create diversions, pulling the enemy away from the main army. During the Wilderness campaign, Grant had sent General Ben Butler with 33,000 men to attack Petersburg. *Beauregard,* with 2,000 men, put up enough resistance at Bermuda Hundred that Butler dug in. By May 16, 1864, when Butler tried to capture Drewry's Bluff, the South had 20,000 men and pushed the Yankees back with heavy losses.

In June, the main body of Grant's troops, a 100,000-man army, began to move southward. For a few days, *Lee* had no idea where Grant was and barely arrived with the main part of his army in time to block Grant's capture of Petersburg. Like lions they faced each other, one too hungry to attack and the other too tired and hot to renew the battle.

Sheridan was sent north and west to pull *Lee's* cavalry away and destroy railroads leading to Richmond. CSA cavalry units, led by *Wade Hampton* and *Fitzhugh Lee,* were able to force Sheridan back from Trevilian Station in June, but not until he had temporarily damaged a railroad.

In July, the eccentric *Jubal Early* was sent north with 8,000 ragged men to pressure Washington to recall all or part of Grant's army. Meeting no opposition at first, the Confederates moved into Maryland, came close enough to Washington's defenses to see the capitol dome, then went on to Pennsylvania where they burned Chambersburg. After *Early* returned to Virginia, Sheridan's troops defeated him at Winchester and Fisher's Hill, but his men returned the favor at Cedar Creek.

At Petersburg, an unusual method of relieving the siege was tried; some Pennsylvania coal miners suggested digging a tunnel to the CSA line and exploding a mine. Burnside supported the plan, but Meade and Grant were less than enthused about its chances of working. A black division was trained for the attack, but at the last minute, Meade ordered that white troops be used. On July 30, 1864, explosives went off, destroying 170 feet of the line and creating a hole 30 feet deep. The white Union soldiers went into the crater rather than around it. The black troops then followed them. When *William Mahone* reorganized his line, the troops in the hole were easy targets, and over 4,000 Union soldiers were killed. Grant called it "a stupendous failure." The siege continued as before.

 *Southern military leaders are in italics.

Name _____

Class _____

POINTS TO CONSIDER

1. As you think about the siege at Petersburg, what missed opportunities did the Union army have that could have shortened it or ended it?

_____

_____

_____

_____

_____

2. Why was Early's raid the cause of so much concern in the North?

_____

_____

_____

_____

_____

3. Imagine yourself as a soldier on either side at the Battle of the Crater. What thoughts would be racing through your mind at such a time?

_____

_____

_____

_____

_____

Name _____

Class _____

CHALLENGES

1. On what did the CSA base its hopes in 1864?

_____

_____

2. Who did Grant send to attack Petersburg?

_____

3. Who blocked Butler's army at Bermuda Hundred?

_____

4. What was the purpose of Sheridan's ride in 1864?

_____

_____

5. What CSA commanders stopped him from doing more damage?

_____

6. What CSA general was sent to draw Yankees away from Petersburg?

_____

7. What northern city did he burn?

_____

8. Who was enthusiastic about the plan to set explosives under the Confederate line at Petersburg?

_____

9. How deep was the crater?

_____

10. What mistake was made by the attacking soldiers?

_____

THE MEETING AT APPOMATTOX

The Surrender at Appomattox

It was April once again, nearly four years since Ft. Sumter; this was the time to plant next year's crop, and for the farmers who made up the bulk of the Confederate army, thoughts were drifting away to home. Some could not resist the temptation to desert; they knew that Grant's army was getting larger, and his supplies were increasing daily. They also knew there was no food for them, and even if they were paid, the money was worthless. Why not go back to take care of family needs? Others were determined to see it through to the end; they had put too much of their lives into this cause to quit before it was over.

To the south, Sherman was meeting organized resistance again. After *Lee* was appointed general in chief, he had reappointed *Joe Johnston* in February 1865 to command an army of 22,000 men against Sherman, now with 90,000 men. As in the past, *Johnston's* tactic was to give ground, but punch whenever a good opportunity presented itself.

Grant's troops kept extending their line around Petersburg, and *Lee* realized that unless he did something soon, his army would be stretched so thin that he would easily be defeated by a sudden Yankee thrust anywhere along the line. Some engagements in the last weeks of the siege at Petersburg were as fierce as any in the war. On March 25, 1865, the Rebels captured Ft. Stedman, a major earthwork on the Union line. The thrill of victory was brief, and the next day most of the Confederates involved were dead, injured, or captured.

The next major engagement was at Five Forks, where Sheridan's cavalry clashed with Rebels on March 30 and April 1. After suffering heavy casualties there, *Lee,* realizing he could no longer hold Petersburg, sent a message to President Davis that he was withdrawing. He then planned his next move. He would head west to Amelia Courthouse on the Richmond & Danville Railroad. Once there, his men would head south to join with *Johnston's* army. The withdrawal did not fool Grant, and Union troops were hot in pursuit, capturing stragglers and supply trains. On April 9, *Lee* knew he was cut off and could not make it to Amelia Courthouse. A time was arranged, and Wilmer McLean's house in Appomattox Courthouse, Virginia, was selected as the place of surrender.

Some of *Lee's* officers wanted to form guerilla units and live off the land, but *Lee* opposed that idea, and they gave in to his wishes. Much has been written about the meeting. *Lee* wore a dress uniform, Grant a dirty coat and mud-covered boots. After small talk about their service together in the Mexican War, *Lee* asked Grant for the terms of surrender and found them to be generous. The Confederates would be paroled, allowed to take their horses and mules home with them, and given 25,000 rations.

As the news spread, there was great joy among the Union soldiers. Then the ragged but proud Army of Northern Virginia stacked their arms, and there was silence as soldiers who had fought so hard now faced each other in peace. For all present, the moment would never be forgotten.

139   *Southern military leaders are in italics.

Name _____

Class _____

POINTS TO CONSIDER

1. Why do you think that all of Lee's army had not deserted by April 1865?

_____

_____

_____

_____

_____

2. What would have happened if Lee's soldiers had broken up in small bands and carried on guerilla warfare?

_____

_____

_____

_____

3. Grant was following Lincoln's directions when he offered generous terms to Lee. What do you think was the reason for Lincoln's policy?

_____

_____

_____

_____

Name _____

Class _____

CHALLENGES

1. What reasons did Confederate deserters have for leaving?

_____

2. Who was back in charge of CSA forces to the south?

_____

3. What fort on the Petersburg line was captured by the Confederates in March?

_____

4. What happened to the troops that captured that fort?

_____

5. What battle convinced Lee he would have to give up Petersburg?

_____

6. What town did Lee hope to reach?

_____

7. What did Lee hope to do after he reached it?

_____

_____

8. At whose home was the surrender signed?

_____

9. What were the terms of surrender?

_____

_____

10. What was the reaction of the Union soldiers as the Confederate troops stacked their arms?

_____

THE CONFEDERATE GOVERNMENT COLLAPSES

Ruins of the Arsenal in Richmond, Virginia

On April 2, 1865, there was a rush of activity as government officials in Richmond scurried around closing up their offices, then raced home to pack their bags and arrange for transportation out of town. If they had had time to reflect that day, they would have wondered what had happened to the enthusiasm and confidence so often expressed just four years before. So many hopes had been held back in 1861. The North would let the South go without a fight. If a war occurred, one Rebel could whip 10 Yankees. Then they pinned their hopes on the superior generalship of Lee and Jackson. The blockade could be broken with an ironclad ripping holes in wooden Union ships. England would come to help because their textile mills would be starved for Confederate cotton. So many dreams had not been realized.

It is easier to spot the mistakes of the past than it is to prevent them from happening in our own time. Let's look back to see where some of the mistakes were that led to the Confederate government moving from Richmond to Danville, North Carolina, where it spent the last few days of its existence. The mistakes are not listed in order of importance, but in the approximate order that they occurred.

1. The CSA had underestimated Lincoln. He was a country lawyer with little national experience. He was not much of a public speaker, yet people understood him. He seemed slow to make decisions, but once they were made, he usually picked the best way to go.

2. In the early days of the blockade, it was very easy to get supplies through. It would have been an ideal time to bring in far more arms, gunpowder, medicine, and other vital items than the CSA actually did. After losing Port Royal, Norfolk, New Orleans, and Mobile Bay, the South was running short on good ports through which supplies could be delivered.

3. "King Cotton diplomacy" assumed that if England and France were cut off from southern cotton, they would fight their way through the blockade to get it. If cotton had been sold overseas, the South could have bought more of the equipment and supplies it needed and been able to pay for them in gold.

4. The decision not to tax put a burden on the public far worse than any reasonable tax could. When money became worthless and people were forced to barter, their opinion of the government must have suffered.

5. The doctrine of states' rights had given a motive for leaving the U.S., but extremists like Vice President Alexander Stephens and Georgia's governor, Joe Brown, were blind to the necessity of putting unity first, and then, after the war, rearranging the government to allow more freedom for states.

6. Slaves were counted on to help win the war, and during the war there were no massive slave rebellions, but work slowed down to a near stop on many farms as slaves waited for some Yankee officer to ride over the hill and tell them they were free. General Patrick Cleburne concluded that blacks might make as good soldiers in gray as in blue uniforms. However, it was naturally difficult for the CSA to accept such a notion after telling themselves for centuries that blacks were inferior.

Name _____

Class _____

POINTS TO CONSIDER

1. What other reasons can you think of that might explain the South's defeat?

_____

_____

_____

_____

_____

2. Which of the reasons given seems to be the most important reason to you?

_____

_____

_____

_____

3. Which reasons would have been the easiest to avoid? Which the hardest to avoid? Why?

_____

_____

_____

_____

Name _____

Class _____

CHALLENGES

1. Why was there so much activity on April 2, 1865?

_____

_____

2. What was the first hope of 1861 to fail?

_____

3. To what city did the Confederates move the government?

_____

4. Why did southerners think Lincoln would be easy to handle?

_____

_____

5. What needed outside supplies were brought through the blockade?

_____

6. Why did the decision *not* to tax hurt loyalty to the CSA?

_____

_____

7. What was the idea behind "King Cotton diplomacy"?

_____

_____

8. How did Alexander Stephens and Joe Brown make the job of winning the war harder?

_____

_____

9. How did slaves hurt the Confederacy, even when they did not revolt?

_____

_____

10. Who suggested bringing black soldiers into the Confederate army?

LINCOLN IS ASSASSINATED

Courtesy New-York Historical Society
John Wilkes Booth

For a man who has witnessed a hard-fought struggle end in victory, Lincoln was in a strange, somber mood. He had often been in these moods since his son, Willie, had died in 1862. On several occasions in 1865, he mentioned premonitions that he would die soon.

John Wilkes Booth was an actor, more famous for dramatic actions on the stage than for the way he delivered lines. A Confederate sympathizer, he wanted to do something dramatic to turn the war around. His original plan was to capture Lincoln and use him as a hostage until southern prisoners of war were returned. He brought several men into his plot, but by April 1865, some had lost interest in the scheme.

The news of the fall of Richmond and Lee's surrender hit Booth hard; a more desperate way to help the South would have to be found. The idea came of killing Lincoln, Vice President Andrew Johnson, and Secretary of State Seward. This would throw the Union government into chaos, and perhaps the CSA could reorganize resistance. When he checked his mail at Ford's Theater on April 14, he was told that Lincoln would attend the evening's performance of *Our American Cousin.* Booth called his little band of followers together and handed out assignments. George Atzerodt was to kill Johnson, and Lewis Powell was to kill Seward. Booth reserved the honor of assassinating Lincoln for himself. After a few drinks at a saloon, Booth went to the theater and made his final preparations for his most dramatic performance.

Mr. and Mrs. Lincoln had planned on taking General and Mrs. Grant with them to the play, but the Grants were not going to be in town. Instead, they took Major Henry Rathbone and his fiancée, Clara Harris. The bodyguard for the evening was John Parker, who left his seat outside the presidential box to find a seat where he could watch the play.

Booth entered the theater after the play had begun, found the president's box un-guarded, and came up behind Lincoln with a Derringer in one hand and a knife in the other. He shot the president at pointblank range and prepared to leap from the box. Rathbone grabbed his arm, and Booth slashed him with the knife. Then Booth jumped, but as he fell, he caught his spur in the bunting draped from the box. He landed off-balance and broke his leg; as he staggered across the stage, he said *"Sic semper tyrannis"* (meaning "Thus always to tyrants") hobbled out the stage door, and rode off.

The other assassins failed in their tasks. Atzerodt never made any effort to kill Johnson, and Powell's efforts to stab Seward failed because he was wearing a heavy collar while recovering from a carriage accident.

Booth escaped to Maryland with a fellow conspirator, David Herold. After getting his leg set by Dr. Samuel Mudd, the two rode off. They were surrounded by Union cavalry, and Booth was killed. Atzerodt, Herold, Powell, and Mrs. Mary Surratt (landlady of the boarding house where the plot was hatched) were hanged.

Name _____

Class _____

POINTS TO CONSIDER

1. Even if Booth's plan had worked, and all the men on the list had been killed, do you think it could have saved the South from defeat? Why?

_____

_____

_____

_____

_____

2. How would you, as a northerner, feel about the South after hearing the news that Lincoln had died?

_____

_____

_____

_____

3. The trial of the conspirators was quick, and the punishments were harsh. If the current president were killed in such a plot, do you think the murderers would receive a fair trial? Why or why not?

_____

_____

_____

_____

Name _____

Class _____

CHALLENGES

1. Why did Booth feel so miserable in April 1865?

_____

_____

2. What had he wanted to do to Lincoln before that time?

_____

_____

3. What other officials besides Lincoln were on the list to be killed?

_____

4. Who was assigned to kill the vice president?

_____

5. Who had the Lincolns planned to take to the theater that night?

_____

6. What army officer attended with the Lincolns?

_____

7. What caused Booth to break his leg?

_____

8. What quotation did Booth give on the stage?

_____

9. Who set Booth's leg?

_____

10. How many were hanged for their part in the conspiracy?

_____

THE IMPACT OF THE WAR

In 1939, the movie *Gone With the Wind* was released, and millions of Americans were caught up in the Civil War once again. A few older Americans had faint memories of the war, and that might explain the interest. But in 1992, the Ken Burns series, *The Civil War,* was televised and got very high ratings as millions of Americans renewed interest in the war. Some have never lost enthusiasm for the war, as shown by subscriptions to magazines relating to the war. Confederate battle flags are still displayed and sometimes debated. Tourists flock to Gettysburg, Antietam, and other battle sites. No other war has ever caught the nation's imagination so thoroughly. Students may not remember when the War of 1812 was fought, or who the Mexican War's opponent was, but names like Lincoln, Lee, Grant, and Jackson are familiar to almost everyone.

Americans have an emotional tie to the war. For sheer drama, the Civil War offered some of the greatest moments in history. The slug fest between the *Merrimac* and *Monitor,* secret orders discovered wrapped around cigars, Pickett's charge at Gettysburg, the last full-scale cavalry battle at Brandy Station, the cadet's charge at New Market, and the Battle of the Crater at Petersburg are only a few from hundreds of examples.

The leaders of the Civil War have become legendary. Rarely does a year go by without a new biography of Lincoln being published. Few traveling in the South dare criticize Robert E. Lee. An admirer wrote in *Confederate Veteran* (March, 1920): "There is seemingly no character in all history that combines power and virtue and charm as he does." If any Yankees doubt that view is still held, just ask any devoted southerner. Surround these "legends" with cavalry officers like J.E.B. Stuart, John Mosby, and Phil Sheridan, or naval officers like Rafael Semmes or David Farragut, or field commanders like Grant, Sherman, or Jackson, and there are enough legendary leaders around to satisfy anyone.

Wilmer McLean's house in Appomattox Courthouse, Virginia, where the terms of surrender were signed by Generals Lee and Grant on April 9, 1865.

148

Obviously the war has affected the nation. Consider some of the effects. It changed the South forever. The destruction caused by the war forced the South to begin a rebuilding process that took much of its energy for the rest of the 19th century. Southern pride was lost for many years after the war, but today no section of the U.S. takes more pride in its regional heritage than the South. The war ended slavery, but the tensions in race relations still linger.

The North was also changed. Industry moved from small shops to large factories, from businessmen with an eye on the local market to those who thought in terms of national markets. A new breed of men was formed by the war: admirers called them "captains of industry," but they would soon be labeled "robber barons." Even in agriculture, the small farmer who tried to get by without expensive equipment was doomed to lose out to his neighbor equipped with the latest thresher, planter, or harvester.

The Civil War would change the course of westward expansion. The transcontinental railroad opened new areas for agriculture, and the Homestead Act made it possible for settlers to occupy the land.

The presidency has been affected by the examples that Lincoln set during the Civil War, and every president since Lincoln has quoted him. When Lincoln took office, he had only a few strong presidents he could model: Washington, Jefferson, Jackson, and Polk. He took charge in ways they never did and set examples that 20th century presidents have followed.

Dedication of a monument on the Bull Run battlefield, June 1865. For many, ceremonies such as this were a first step in putting the war behind them.

ANSWERS TO CHALLENGES

The unanswered question: the meaning of Union (page 3)
1. Nullify means to cancel.
2. Defender: John C. Calhoun.
3. Phrase used by Daniel Webster.
4. Farming: South.
5. Business: North.
6. Aristocrats called planters.
7. Missouri Compromise put together by Henry Clay.
8. Line drawn at 36°30'.
9. Jefferson saw it as alarm like a fire-bell.
10. Abolitionist opposed colonizing and slavery.

The South: old times were not forgotten (page 6)
1. Slave states covered 896,000 square miles.
2. Maryland and Virginia: tobacco.
3. Missouri: hemp and corn.
4. Louisiana: sugar.
5. Most highly valued: cotton.
6. Wealthiest: planters.
7. Owned 20 or more slaves: 46,274.
8. Owned 500 or more: 11.
9. Lawyers and ministers tied to them through money.
10. They refused to do the work of slaves.

The North before the war: expanding frontiers (page 9)
1. Indiana: 4.
2. New England agriculture declined.
3. Inventions: steel plow, reaper, threshing machine, and corn planter among others.
4. Buildings: elevator.
5. Cities: New York, Philadelphia, Baltimore.
6. Over 2,000 miles of railroad: 5 states. [In comparison, Virginia led South with 1,700 miles]
7. Railroads better equipped and maintained.
8. Telegraph: Samuel F.B. Morse.
9. Line: 50,000 miles.
10. Northerners either liked it or saw it as inevitable.

Controversies: Wilmot to "Bleeding Kansas" (page 12)
1. No.
2. Proposed exclusion: David Wilmot.
3. Southerners warned they might secede.
4. Land: 529,000 square miles.
5. Reason: gold discovered in California.
6. Most important: Henry Clay and Stephen Douglas.
7. Southern critics: Jefferson Davis and John C. Calhoun.
8. Woman: Harriet Beecher Stowe.
9. Kansas-Nebraska: Stephen Douglas.
10. Destroyed Whigs, split Democrats, created Republicans.

ANSWERS TO CHALLENGES (continued)

Dred Scott to John Brown 1857-1859 (page 15)
1. Days: 3.
2. Taney: neither.
3. Territories existed for common use and equal benefit of all.
4. Opponent: Abraham Lincoln.
5. Most famous: Freeport.
6. Could keep slavery out by passing unfriendly laws.
7. Douglas went to Senate.
8. Brown had murdered 5 men and boys in Kansas.
9. Harpers Ferry had a federal arsenal.
10. Lincoln feared Brown had gone too far.

The 1860 election and the secession crisis (page 18)
1. Northern Democrats: Stephen Douglas.
2. Blocking him: opposition from South.
3. Constitutional Union: Whigs and Know-Nothings.
4. CU candidate: John Bell.
5. Northern Democrat: Douglas.
6. Southern Democrat: John Breckinridge.
7. Campaigner: Douglas.
8. Lincoln: 180 electoral votes.
9. Problems: felt had no right to force states to remain, disloyalty.
10. Forts: Sumter and Pickens.

Sumter forces decisions in the Upper South (page 21)
1. Commander: Major Robert Anderson.
2. CSA commander: P.G.T. Beauregard.
3. Tried to convince border states.
4. Shelling: 4:30 a.m. on April 12, 1861.
5. Requested 75,000.
6. Should suggest that he thought war would be short.
7. Ellis: would not participate against South.
8. Magoffin: wanted Kentucky to be neutral.
9. Lincoln had 19 Maryland legislators arrested.
10. Jackson: South.

War leaders compared: Lincoln vs. Davis (page 24)
1. Davis educated at Transylvania and West Point.
2. Served in Mexican War.
3. Had been senator and secretary of war.
4. Lincoln: lawyer.
5. Lincoln in Black Hawk War.
6. Job: Member of Congress for one term.
7. Lincoln walked streets without a bodyguard.
8. Davis: tried to put down a riot by himself.
9. Lincoln waited until public opinion supported policy.
10. Lincoln visited military hospitals and talked to citizens.

ANSWERS TO CHALLENGES (continued)

Enthusiasm for war runs high in North and South (page 27)
1. South talked about "Battle Summer."
2. War: American Revolution.
3. Least killed: Mexican War.
4. European war: Crimean War.
5. Age: 17-21.
6. Youngest brevet: Galusha Pennypacker.
7. Youngest Confederate: William Roberts.
8. Generals in 40s: Sherman, Meade, Hooker.
9. Confederates in 30s: Pickett, Jackson.
10. Fez: Zouave.

Organizing the two armies (page 30)
1. Territorial Department: named after the area where the army would be used.
2. Union: named after major river flowing where they operated.
3. CSA: named after state or region where operated.
4. Units organized in towns: big battles killed many local men.
5. Companies elected officers.
6. Regiment commanded by colonel.
7. Cavalry regiment: 12 companies.
8. CSA brigades: named after commanding officer.
9. Two or more brigades made up division.
10. At least 2, and often 3 divisions made up corps.

The instruments of war: infantry, cavalry, artillery (page 33)
1. Backbone: infantry.
2. Book: Manual of Arms. [Both used Hardee's *Rifle and Light Infantry Tactics*.]
3. End of charge most critical; ended with hand-to-hand combat.
4. Artillery broke up charges and was used during sieges. [Also used to soften enemy in preparation for a charge.]
5. Canister: little iron balls fired from a cannon.
6. Range: 1,500-2,500 yards.
7. Cavalryman: revolver, saber, carbine.
8. Eyes: used to scout enemy positions.
9. Cavalry could be used to quickly plug holes in line. Would dismount and fight like infantry.
10. Charge: no.

Arms of the Civil War (page 36)
1. Technology advances because each side wants an advantage over the other.
2. Rifleman's war because infantryman and his rifle usually decided who would win battles.
3. Breechloader easier to fire and faster to reload.
4. Officers afraid men would waste ammunition.
5. President Lincoln tested rifles.
6. Soldiers with revolvers: officers, cavalrymen, and some artillerymen.
7. Artillery: 3-inch rifle and Napoleon guns.
8. Range up to 5,000 yards.
9. Ships sunk: 32.
10. Modern because of new weapons and new tactics to make full use of them.

ANSWERS TO CHALLENGES (continued)

Bull Run: the first major test of the war (page 39)
1. Because they were the capitals.
2. Manassas important railroad center.
3. North in hurry: 90-day enlistments running out.
4. McDowell slow because troops soft and weather hot.
5. General Bee said he was standing like a stone wall.
6. Johnston moved troops by rail.
7. Tried small attacks rather than a mass attack.
8. Problem with sightseers and picnickers getting in the way.
9. Jackson's brigade was joined by three retreating brigades.
10. Johnston's men too tired and disorganized to follow.

CSA makes major decisions (page 42)
1. Resembled U.S. Constitution.
2. President Jefferson Davis
3. Vice President Alexander Stephens.
4. City: Richmond.
5. Color: cadet gray.
6. Dyed with boiled nut shells and iron oxide filings.
7. First flag: Stars and Bars.
8. Suggestion: Beauregard.
9. Banner looked like truce flag when there was no wind.
10. Printed money without any backing.

Welles vs. Mallory: battle of the blockade (page 45)
1. Coastline 3,550 miles long.
2. Area: about 84.5 miles each.
3. Reason: keep arms and supplies from coming in.
4. Base: Port Royal.
5. CSA: Stephen Mallory.
6. Name: *Merrimac.*
7. Submarine: *Hunley.*
8. Victim: *Housatonic.*
9. Semmes: *Alabama.*
10. Around world: *Shenandoah.*

Ft. Henry and Ft. Donelson: Grant's rising star (page 48)
1. Rivers cut into western part of Confederacy.
2. Gunboats: Flag Officer Andrew Foote.
3. Waters brought them up to level of fort, so easier to attack.
4. Capture: 2 hours.
5. Donelson much higher and guns couldn't reach high enough to do much damage.
6. CSA commanders: Gideon Pillow, John Floyd, Simon Buckner.
7. Charge: Nathan Bedford Forrest.
8. Failed because Pillow turned around and retreated to fort.
9. Surrender: Buckner.
10. Terms: unconditional surrender.

Merrimac vs. the *Monitor*: battle of the ironclads (page 51)
1. Official: Stephen Mallory.
2. Renamed the *Virginia*.
3. Changed by heavy iron plates covering it; armed with 10 heavy cannons capable of firing 100-pound shells.
4. Secretary of the Navy: Gideon Welles.
5. Designer: John Ericsson.
6. Date: January 30, 1862.
7. Sailors doing their laundry.
8. Sank 2 (*Cumberland* and *Congress*).
9. Battle at Hampton Roads, Virginia.
10. Destroyed: *Virginia (Merrimac)*; Storm: *Monitor*.

McClellan's Peninsular Campaign of 1862 (page 54)
1. Replaced Winfield Scott.
2. Planned to take troops by ship to James Peninsula.
3. Divisions: 12.
4. First: Magruder.
5. Mistake: had more men than Magruder and could have broken through.
6. Dividing troops: Chickahominy River.
7. Reason: Johnston was wounded.
8. Sent to scout: Jeb Stuart.
9. Lee knew McClellan was very cautious.
10. Men: 70,000.

The Seven Days Battle (page 57)
1. Led V Corps: A.P. Hill.
2. Porter destroyed bridge.
3. McClellan burned supplies.
4. Malvern Hill on high plateau; good strategic position.
5. Defended Malvern Hill: Fitz-John Porter.
6. Cannons: 250.
7. Described: D.H. Hill.
8. Excuse: he was outnumbered.
9. McClellan had 55,000 more men.
10. Characteristics: willing to take risk, and developed strategy to meet opponent's personality.

The Confederate High Command (page 60)
1. General: Joseph Johnston.
2. Towns: Jubal Early.
3. Stuart in cavalry.
4. Stuart rode circles around them.
5. Jackson teaching at Virginia Military Institute (VMI).
6. Jackson killed at Chancellorsville.
7. Father was Revolutionary War hero (Lighthorse Harry Lee).
8. Statement: no.
9. Right arm: Stonewall Jackson.
10. Disliked Early: Grant.

ANSWERS TO CHALLENGES (continued)

The Battle of New Orleans (page 63)
1. It would split the Confederacy in two.
2. Island No. 10 located at New Madrid, Missouri.
3. Forts: Jackson and St. Philip.
4. Hulls of ships had been tied together in harbor.
5. Gave away presence: the moon came out.
6. Resistance: none at New Orleans.
7. Other cities: Baton Rouge and Natchez.
8. Vicksburg located on bluff 300 feet above river, and could not aim guns high enough.
9. Farragut promoted to rear admiral.
10. Appointee: Ben Butler.

The Border War (page 66)
1. Border state support could affect outcome of war.
2. Lincoln sent troops to state to sway public and legislature.
3. Kentucky declared itself neutral.
4. Leonidas Polk (CSA) moved troops into Kentucky.
5. Grant occupied Paducah and Southland.
6. General ordered in: Albert Sidney Johnston.
7. Served in southern army: 35,000.
8. Jackson refused to send troops and tried to seize arsenal at St. Louis.
9. Winning general: Sterling Price.
10. Union victory: Pea Ridge, Arkansas.

The Battle at Shiloh Church (page 69)
1. CSA commander: Albert Johnston.
2. He wanted to attack before Buell's men arrived.
3. Union officers: William T. Sherman and Ben Prentiss.
4. Nickname: Hornet's Nest.
5. Killed: Johnston. Took charge: Beauregard.
6. Union army received reinforcements.
7. Withdrew because could not get support he needed from Van Dorn.
8. Discouraged pursuit: Nathan Forrest.
9. 3,400 killed (about even for both sides).
10. Wounded: 16,000 (also about even).

A hot day at Antietam Creek (page 72)
1. The South hoped to be recognized by England or France and receive financial help.
2. Special Order 191 was found wrapped around cigars.
3. McClellan had 36,000 more men.
4. Jackson away attacking Harpers Ferry.
5. Hood was attacked in a cornfield north of Sharpsburg.
6. General killed: Mansfield.
7. Sunken road known as "Bloody Lane."
8. Named after Burnside who worked so hard to take it.
9. Stopped advance: A.P. Hill.
10. Killed: 4,100; wounded: 18,500.

ANSWERS TO CHALLENGES (continued)

Medical Care in the Civil War (page 75)
1. Medical officers: 115; joined Confederate army: 22.
2. Wore title of surgeon general: 4.
3. Little known about Confederate medical corps because records were destroyed.
4. Leading cause: disease.
5. Most common: measles and mumps.
6. Places: colleges, warehouses, hotels, railroad depots.
7. First field hospital: Shiloh.
8. Wounds treated by amputation.
9. Private agency: U.S. Sanitary Commission.
10. Largest hospital: Chimborazo at Richmond.

Fredericksburg: a Christmas present for Lee (page 78)
1. General replaced: McClellan.
2. River: Rappahannock.
3. Under Lee: Jackson and Longstreet.
4. Burnside's commanders: Sumner, Hooker, and Franklin.
5. Delayed by not receiving pontoons.
6. Longstreet's men in sunken road behind stone wall.
7. Misery: snow, sleet, and cold.
8. Beaten back 7 times.
9. Wanted to continue: Burnside.
10. Union lost 7,400 more men.

The Draft is imposed: South and North (page 81)
1. Age limits: 18-35.
2. 1864 limits: 17-50.
3. Unpopular because gave wealthy chance to avoid draft.
4. Substitutes: $6,000.
5. New group: blacks.
6. Pay $300.
7. 1863 draft: 20-45.
8. Riot: New York City.
9. Brokers hired so would not have to draft men.
10. Quality poor.

Trent affair: tempting England (page 84)
1. *Trent* was mail packet.
2. Diplomats: James Mason and John Slidell.
3. Captain Charles Wilkes.
4. Captain furious but could do little to stop them.
5. Saw U.S. as strong competitor; would be weakened if broken in two.
6. Spokesman: John Bright.
7. Persuaded: Prince Albert.
8. Demanded Mason and Slidell be released, and U.S. apologize to Great Britain.
9. Release: Yes.
10. Accomplished nothing.

ANSWERS TO CHALLENGES (continued)

Congress creates a new future for the nation (page 87)
1. Committee: Radical Republicans.
2. Democrat: Clement Vallandigham.
3. Arrest: General [Ambrose] Burnside.
4. Morrill tariff raised it.
5. Excise: special tax on some luxuries.
6. Nickname: greenbacks.
7. Land: 160 acres.
8. Had to wait 5 years.
9. Railroads: Central Pacific and Union Pacific.
10. Northern Pacific: Lake Superior to Portland.

Entertainment during the war (page 90)
1. Poets: Tennyson and Longfellow.
2. Magazine: *Police Gazette*.
3. Dime Novels: Erastus Beadle.
4. Performer: Tom Thumb.
5. Black performer "Blind Tom."
6. Union: "Battle Hymn of Republic."
7. Confederate: "Dixie."
8. Pitcher 45 feet away.
9. Home plate was round.
10. Snowball fight: 5,000 men.

Civilians do their part in the war (page 93)
1. Beauregard's spy: Rose Greenhow.
2. Jackson's spy: Belle Boyd.
3. Elizabeth Van Lew and Mary Bowser.
4. Agency: Pinkerton
5. Superintendent of Nurses: Dorothea Dix.
6. Nurse: Clara Barton.
7. Medal: Dr. Mary Walker.
8. Fairs: U.S. Sanitary Commission.
9. Group: Christian Commission.
10. Sisters of Charity supplied nurses.

Civil rights in the North during the war (page 96)
1. Habeas corpus: Article 1, Section 9.
2. Protects your right to go to court and have charges read against you.
3. City: Baltimore.
4. Merryman: burning bridges and cutting telegraph lines.
5. Judge: Taney.
6. Officer: commander at Ft. McHenry.
7. Newspapers: jail editor or refuse to mail them.
8. Pringle was sent home.
9. Objectors could be used in hospitals, take care of freedmen, or pay $300 for care of sick and wounded.
10. Probably no.

ANSWERS TO CHALLENGES (continued)

Freeing the blacks and letting them fight (page 99)
1. Congress said purpose was to save Union.
2. Lincoln: loyal border states would oppose it.
3. Abolitionists wanted slaves freed.
4. Purvis opposed colonizing.
5. Lincoln would pay $400.
6. Rejected offer.
7. Emancipation Proclamation: January 1, 1863.
8. Recruiter: Lorenzo Thomas.
9. West: Milliken's Bend, Mississippi.
10. East: Ft. Wagner, South Carolina.

Chancellorsville: Hooker's lesson in warfare (page 102)
1. Nickname: "Fighting Joe."
2. Lincoln saw army had defeatist spirit.
3. Hooker: "Finest army on the planet."
4. At Fredericksburg: John Sedgwick.
5. Discovered it: Jeb Stuart.
6. Flank move: 26,000.
7. It left Lee with 17,000 men to face Hooker's whole army.
8. Jackson shot by one of own men while riding back from survey of enemy positions.
9. Jackson died.
10. Lee's army drove Sedgwick back.

Vicksburg: the rock that finally fell (page 105)
1. Fortified: 50 miles.
2. Naval officer: David Farragut.
3. Messed up: Van Dorn and Forrest.
4. Sherman: Chickasaw Bluffs.
5. Grant thought it was better to keep the men working than loafing and getting soft.
6. Cavalry: Ben Grierson.
7. At Jackson: Joe Johnston.
8. Forced to eat horses, mules, dogs, cats, muskrats.
9. Reasons: out of food and could not defend against strong attack.
10. Prisoners: 31,600.

Gettysburg: the accidental battle (page 108)
1. Longstreet wanted to help Bragg in the Chattanooga area.
2. Lee wanted to invade Pennsylvania and force Federal troops in the West to be pulled east.
3. In charge: Joe Hooker.
4. Cavalry battle: Brandy Station.
5. Stuart to harrass the Yankees, destroy supplies, and gather information.
6. Hooker wanted to attack Richmond.
7. Lincoln wanted to destroy Lee's army.
8. George Meade replaced Hooker.
9. Hill interested in seizing the shoes that were stored there.
10. Supporting Buford: John Reynolds; supporting Hill: Richard Ewell.

ANSWERS TO CHALLENGES (continued)

Gettysburg: showdown at Cemetery Ridge (page 111)
1. Lee felt he must fight or retreat.
2. Meade concerned because Confederates could use it to attack Washington.
3. Sickles left gap between Union line and Little Round Top.
4. Lee hoped that with one big push he could break Federal spirit.
5. Longstreet opposed Pickett's Charge.
6. Ewell's troops were driven off Culp's Hill.
7. 258 cannons involved.
8. Charge: 10,500 men.
9. Meade felt men were too tired.
10. Lincoln not pleased.

The Union high command: Grant in charge (page 114)
1. Both had been sent west, away from the war.
2. Burnside and Hooker both working for Grant.
3. Quartermaster general supplies troops with clothing, supplies, and food.
4. Henry Halleck had responsibility.
5. Qualities: deep thought, extreme determination, great simplicity and calmness.
6. Critics: reputation for drinking, poor grammar, and inability to march in step.
7. Halleck explained military affairs to civilians.
8. Sherman opposed stealing, robbery, and pillage.
9. Most colorful: Custer.
10. Five generals became president: Grant, Hayes, Garfield, Arthur, and Benjamin Harrison.

From the Wilderness to Cold Harbor (page 117)
1. Rank: lieutenant general.
2. Grant to design all Union strategy.
3. Promised that whatever happened, would not turn back.
4. Union could not make full use of cavalry and artillery advantage.
5. Wounded: Longstreet.
6. Stopped fighting to rescue wounded from brush fires.
7. Successful: Emory Upton and Winfield Hancock.
8. Fighting: Bloody Angle.
9. Pinned names to make easier to identify bodies.
10. Grant suffered heavy casualties.

Sherman takes Atlanta and marches through Georgia (page 120)
1. Worked together at Ft. Henry and Ft. Donelson.
2. Sherman promoted because of Grant's new job.
3. City: Atlanta.
4. CSA commander: Joe Johnston.
5. Battles: Dalton, Resaca, Cassville, and Kennesaw Mountain.
6. Bragg and Hood persuaded Davis.
7. Hood: by attacking Sherman before he got to Atlanta defenses.
8. Cavalryman: Joe Wheeler.
9. Sherman ordered city evacuated and set fire to it.
10. City: Savannah.

ANSWERS TO CHALLENGES (continued)

Let us have peace, NOW! (page 123)
1. Argument: if Lincoln hadn't been elected, would have been no war.
2. Nickname: copperheads.
3. Group: Knights of the Golden Circle (KGC).
4. Truth: Yes.
5. Wolf: would be better if they were dead.
6. South: Heroes of America.
7. Newspaper: *North Carolina Standard.*
8. Met with Adams: Thomas Yeatman.
9. Talks failed because Yeatman had no authority.
10. Editor: Horace Greeley.

The Lincoln Cabinet: internal civil war (page 126)
1. Seward: New York.
2. Offices: governor and senator.
3. Trouble: statements he had made.
4. Chase: governor and senator.
5. Chase self-righteous and humorless.
6. Rumors: Seward
7. Stanton: Democrat.
8. Battle: Fredericksburg.
9. Seward accused of being lukewarm in conduct of war.
10. Lincoln: to tell senators Cabinet always consulted, and Cabinet there to confirm it.

The election of 1864: Lincoln vs. McClellan (page 129)
1. Critics: Ben Wade and Samuel Pomeroy.
2. Pomeroy favored Chase.
3. Other: Frémont.
4. Policies: continuing the war and peace.
5. Democrat: George McClellan.
6. Sheridan succeeded in Shenandoah Valley and let 10,000 soldiers go home to vote.
7. Custer displayed captured battle flags.
8. 200 electoral votes.
9. House: 105.
10. Senate 31.

Civilian life in the North during the war (page 132)
1. Borden: condensed milk.
2. Rockefeller: oil refining.
3. Cotton: Andrew Butler.
4. Howard: gold.
5. Speculator would want to lose.
6. Farmers: yes.
7. Blacks: unpopular because were used as strikebreakers.
8. Newspaper: New York *Tribune.*
9. Publisher: Horace Greeley.
10. Couple: Tom Thumb, Lavinia Warren.

ANSWERS TO CHALLENGES (continued)

The South during the war: doing without (page 135)
1. Riot: Richmond.
2. Stopped it: Jefferson Davis.
3. Easy because no police, sheriffs, or judges.
4. Most crime: mountains, swamps, and remote areas.
5. Memminger: tax to raise money.
6. Congress paid for it by loans and printing paper money.
7. Company: Erlanger & Co.
8. Stopped because of battle defeats at Gettysburg and Vicksburg.
9. About 175,000 to 200,000.
10. Most welcome: teachers, ministers, and physicians.

Petersburg is besieged (page 138)
1. Hopes: Lincoln would lose election to McClellan.
2. Grant sent Butler.
3. Blocked Butler: Beauregard.
4. Sheridan to draw Lee's troops away and destroy railroads.
5. CSA commanders: Wade Hampton and Fitzhugh Lee.
6. CSA: Jubal Early.
7. City: Chambersburg, Pennsylvania.
8. Enthusiastic: Burnside.
9. Crater 30 feet deep.
10. Troops went into crater rather than around it.

The meeting at Appomatox (page 141)
1. Deserter reasons: no food, worthless pay, need to go home and take care of family.
2. In charge: Joe Johnston.
3. Fort captured: Ft. Stedman.
4. Most were killed, injured, or captured.
5. Battle: Five Forks.
6. Hoped to reach Amelia Courthouse.
7. Hoped to take train south to join Johnston's army.
8. Home of Wilmer McLean.
9. Terms: soldiers paroled, allowed to take horses and mules, and given 25,000 rations.
10. Soldiers were silent.

The Confederate government collapses (page 144)
1. Activity: Lee informed Davis could no longer hold at Petersburg.
2. First hope: that North would allow South to leave without a war.
3. Moved capital to Danville, North Carolina.
4. Lincoln was country lawyer with little national experience.
5. Supplies: arms, gunpowder, medicine.
6. Money worthless, and people forced to barter.
7. King Cotton: cut off cotton, and England and France would have to fight way through blockade to get it.
8. Stephens and Brown insisted on states' rights.
9. Slaves didn't work very hard.
10. Suggestion to let slaves fight: General Patrick Cleburne.

ANSWERS TO CHALLENGES (continued)

Lincoln is assassinated (page 147)
1. Richmond had fallen.
2. Booth planned to kidnap Lincoln.
3. List: Johnson and Seward.
4. Vice president to be killed by George Atzerodt.
5. Planned to take Grants.
6. Attended: Major Henry Rathbone.
7. Booth caught spur in bunting.
8. Quote: "Sic Semper Tyrannus."
9. Leg set by Dr. Samuel Mudd.
10. Hanged: 4.

ANSWERS TO THE BRAGGING CONTEST

Page 163	Page 164	Page 165
1. Webster	1. Beauregard	1. Longstreet
2. McCormick	2. McClellan	2. Anderson
3. Douglas	3. Burnside	3. Johnston
4. Scott	4. Cleburne	4. Hood
5. Breckinridge	5. Slidell	5. Copperhead
6. Anderson	6. Barnum	6. Seward
7. Davis	7. Barton	7. McClellan
8. Zouave	8. Merryman	8. Memminger
9. Artilleryman	9. Lincoln	9. Early
10. Minie	10. Hooker	10. Grant
11. McDowell	11. Pemberton	11. Lee
12. Ericsson	12. Meade	12. Stephens
13. Grant	13. Pickett	13. Booth
14. Lee	14. Sherman	14. Atzerodt
15. McClellan	15. Grant	15. Surratt
16. Jackson		
17. Farragut		
18. Lyon		

UNION LEADERS Page 166

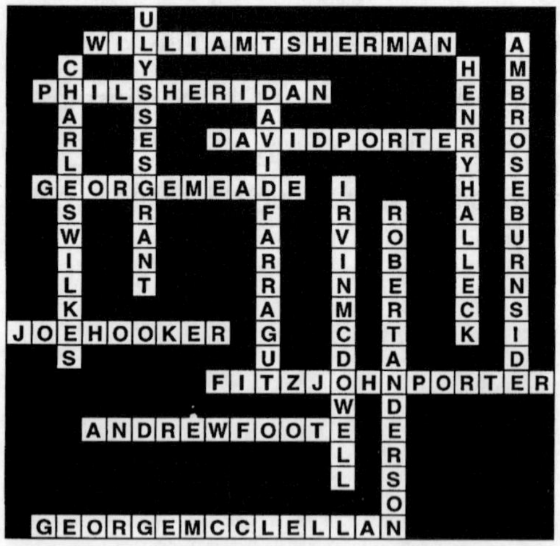

CONFEDERATE LEADERS Page 167

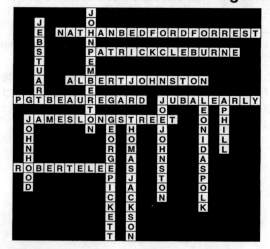

ANSWERS TO "WHOSE ARMY IS THIS?" Page 168 From top to bottom: Army of the Potomac, III Corps, 2nd Division, 1st Brigade, 5th New York Infantry Regiment, Company A. You are in the Union army.

Name _____ **Date** _____

THE BRAGGING CONTEST

At a convention of famous people from the Civil War era, the following people met in a room. The lights went out, and they could only identify themselves by mentioning their accomplishments. Which of those in the group can you identify? Place the correct name from the list below on the line next to that person's accomplishment.

_____ 1. I argued that liberty and union are one.

_____ 2. My mechanical reaper revolutionized agriculture.

_____ 3. I was honored to work with Henry Clay in selling the Compromise of 1850 to Congress.

_____ 4. After my case went to the Supreme Court, I became the most famous slave in America.

_____ 5. I was the southern Democratic candidate in 1860.

_____ 6. I was forced to surrender at Ft. Sumter.

_____ 7. I would have preferred being a general rather than Confederate president.

_____ 8. I had the most unusual uniform in the war.

_____ 9. My canister had a deadly effect on the enemy.

_____ 10. The lead balls fired from muzzleloading rifles were named after me.

_____ 11. Lincoln ordered me to attack at Bull Run.

_____ 12. I designed the North's *Monitor*.

_____ 13. My reputation began with the victories at Ft. Henry and Ft. Donelson.

_____ 14. After Joe Johnston was wounded, I became Confederate commander in Virginia.

_____ 15. Lincoln was very unhappy with me after the Seven Days battle.

_____ 16. I did not live long enough to enjoy the victory at Chancellorsville.

_____ 17. My ships made victory at New Orleans possible.

_____ 18. I lost the battle and my life at Wilson's Creek.

POSSIBLE ANSWERS

Robert Anderson	Artilleryman	John Breckinridge
Jefferson Davis	Stephen Douglas	John Ericsson
David Farragut	Ulysses Grant	Stonewall Jackson
Robert E. Lee	Nathaniel Lyon	George McClellan
Cyrus McCormick	Irvin McDowell	Claude Minie
Dred Scott	Daniel Webster	Zouave

THE BRAGGING CONTEST

At a convention of famous people from the Civil War era, the following people met in a room. The lights went out, and they could only identify themselves by mentioning their accomplishments. Which of those in the group can you identify? Place the correct name from the list below on the line next to that person's accomplishment.

_____ 1. I took over at Shiloh after Johnston died.

_____ 2. I had Lee's orders at Antietam and still failed to defeat him.

_____ 3. My pontoons didn't arrive on time; otherwise, I would have taken Fredericksburg.

_____ 4. I suggested that slaves be brought into the Confederate army as soldiers.

_____ 5. I was captured and dragged off the *Trent.*

_____ 6. General Tom Thumb worked for me.

_____ 7. After serving as a nurse in the war, I went on to head the American Red Cross.

_____ 8. Even the chief justice couldn't get me released from a military prison.

_____ 9. I signed the Emancipation Proclamation.

_____ 10. I commanded the finest army on the planet, but lost at Chancellorsville.

_____ 11. I blame my loss at Vicksburg on Joe Johnston.

_____ 12. If I had heard my troops calling me a "snapping turtle," I'd have shot them.

_____ 13. I led the most famous charge of the war.

_____ 14. I advised Grant not to get involved in Washington politics.

_____ 15. I told my officers not to worry about what Lee was planning, but make their own plans.

POSSIBLE ANSWERS

P. T. Barnum	Clara Barton	P. G. T. Beauregard
Ambrose Burnside	Patrick Cleburne	Ulysses Grant
Joe Hooker	Abraham Lincoln	George McClellan
George Meade	John Merryman	John Pemberton
George Pickett	William T. Sherman	John Slidell

THE BRAGGING CONTEST

At a convention of famous people from the Civil War era, the following people met in a room. The lights went out, and they could only identify themselves by mentioning their accomplishments. Which of those in the group can you identify? Place the correct name from the list below on the line next to that person's accomplishment.

_____ 1. In the Wilderness, I played an important part in beating off the Yankee attack.

_____ 2. My men dug five miles of trenches at Spotsylvania during the Wilderness campaign.

_____ 3. After I was fired, Hood took command of my troops defending Atlanta.

_____ 4. Lee described me as "all lion and no fox."

_____ 5. As a peace Democrat, I was often called this insulting name by Republicans.

_____ 6. I was Lincoln's secretary of state.

_____ 7. I ran against Lincoln in 1864.

_____ 8. I tried to get the CSA Congress to start taxing, but they ignored me.

_____ 9. During the siege of Petersburg, my troops got close enough to Washington to see the capitol building.

_____ 10. I regretted giving approval for that crazy crater scheme at Petersburg.

_____ 11. I was sorry I had to meet with Grant at Appomattox.

_____ 12. As Confederate vice president, I often disagreed with President Davis.

_____ 13. My original plan was to capture Lincoln and use him as a hostage.

_____ 14. I was assigned to kill Vice President Johnson, but did not even try.

_____ 15. Even though I was only the landlady, I was hanged for being involved in the plot to kill the president.

POSSIBLE ANSWERS

Richard Anderson	George Atzerodt	John Wilkes Booth
Copperhead	Jubal Early	Ulysses Grant
John Hood	Joe Johnston	Robert E. Lee
James Longstreet	George McClellan	Christopher Memminger
William Seward	Alexander Stephens	Mary Surratt

UNION LEADERS CROSSWORD PUZZLE

Use the clues below to fill in the names of the Union army leaders in the puzzle.

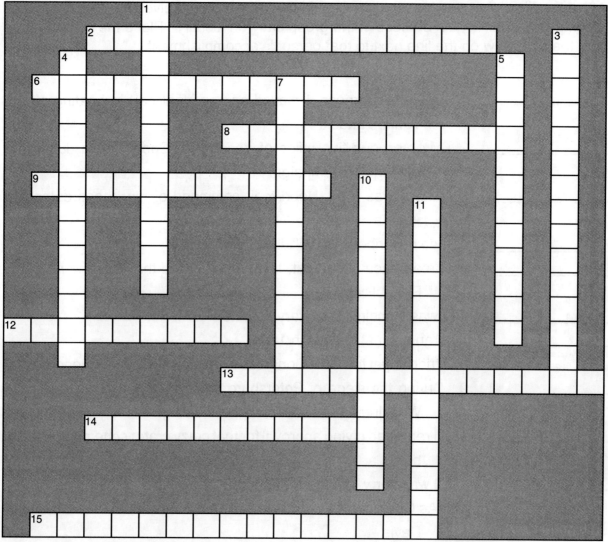

ACROSS

2. He made the "March to the Sea."

6. His cavalry beat Lee to Cold Harbor during the Wilderness Campaign.

8. He was in charge of the fleet that ferried Grant's troops across the river near Vicksburg.

9. He assumed command of the Army of the Potomac three days before Gettysburg.

12. He lead the Army of the Potomac at Chancellorsville.

13. He crossed the Chickahominy River and burned the bridge behind him during the Seven Days battle.

14. He commanded the gunboats during the attacks on Ft. Henry and Ft. Donelson.

15. He was reluctant to move, always thinking the South had a larger army than it did.

DOWN

1. He was nicknamed "Unconditional Surrender" early in the war.

3. He supported the plan that led to the Battle of the Crater.

4. He was captain of the ship that captured the *Trent*.

5. He commanded the Department of the Missouri and explained military strategy to President Lincoln.

7. His gunships were responsible for the capture of New Orleans.

10. He led the Union army at the first Battle of Bull Run.

11. He surrendered Ft. Sumter to the Confederates.

CONFEDERATE LEADERS CROSSWORD PUZZLE

Use the clues below to fill in the names of the Confederate army leaders in the puzzle.

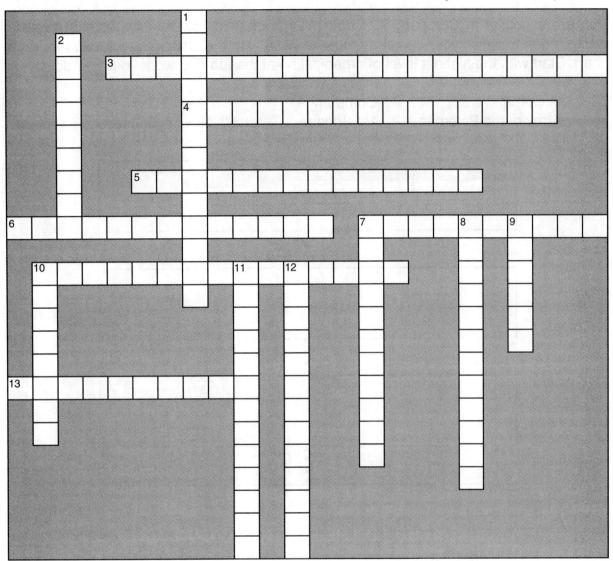

ACROSS

3.   This cavalry leader led an attack at Ft. Donelson.

4. He suggested blacks be allowed to fight in the Confederate army.

5. He decided to attack Grant's forces at Shiloh Church.

6. He directed the firing on Ft. Sumter.

7. During the siege of Petersburg, his men came close enough to Washington to see the capitol dome.

10. He was shot by his own men during the Wilderness Campaign.

13. He was commander of the Army of Northern Virginia for most of the war.

DOWN

1. He was the commander at Vicksburg, Mississippi.

2. He was the cavalry leader at the Battle of Brandy Station, the largest cavalry battle of the war.

7. He was in charge of defending Atlanta, but was relieved of his duties by President Davis.

8. He was the first to break Kentucky's neutrality.

9. His search for shoes at Gettysburg led to a major battle.

10. He burned everything of military value and left Atlanta September 1, 1864.

11.   His division made the famous charge at Gettysburg.

12. He earned the nickname "Stonewall."

WHOSE ARMY IS THIS?

You are a soldier in Company A. Complete the chart below by filling in the levels of organization to which your company must answer. Use the choices provided to fill in the chart. Start with the highest level of organization at the top and work your way down.

III Corps	Company A	2nd Division
Army of the Potomac	1st Brigade	5th New York Infantry Regiment

Using the names of the units as clues, are you in the Union or Confederate army?

BIBLIOGRAPHY

There are thousands of books and articles about the Civil War, and space does not allow a complete list. Many teachers have used the *Official Records of the War of the Rebellion* (OR) in their classes. Many excellent books have been written about the war, and some magazines specialize in the war; a nearby library might have some of them. The following books and articles were used by the authors in preparing this book and give a small sample of what is available for the teacher and student to use. *CWT* stands for *Civil War Times,* which became *CWTI* in 1962, which is *Civil War Times Illustrated. AH* stands for *American Heritage. AHI* stands for *American History Illustrated. JAH* stands for *Journal of American History.*

Books about the antebellum period
Barnes, Gilbert. *The Anti-Slavery Impulse.* New York: Harcourt, Brace & World, 1964.
Current, Richard. *Lincoln and the First Shot.* Philadelphia: Lippincott, 1963.
Hinton, Richard. *John Brown and His Men.* New York: Funk & Wagnalls, 1894.

Articles about the antebellum period
Ehrlich, Walter. "Was the Dred Scott Case Valid?" *JAH,* September, 1968.
Hitchcock, William. "Southern Moderates and Secession." *JAH,* March, 1973.
Holzer, Harry. "Raid on Harper's Ferry." *AHI*, March, 1984.

General books about the Civil War
Boatner, Mark. *Civil War Dictionary.* New York: David McKay, 1959.
Commager, Henry S. *The Blue and the Gray.* New York: Fairfax, 1982.
Guernsey, Alfred and Henry Walden. *Harper's Pictorial History of the Civil War.* Harper, 1866.
McPherson, James. *Ordeal by Fire.* New York: McGraw Hill, 1992.
Nevins, Allan. *The War for the Union.* New York: Scribner's, 1960. 4 volumes.
Randall, J.G. and David Donald. *Civil War and Reconstruction.* Boston: Heath, 1961.
Sifakis, Stewart. *Who was Who in the Civil War.* New York: Oxford, 1988.

Books on specific subjects
Boller, Paul. *Presidential Campaigns.* New York: Oxford, 1985.
Catton, Bruce. *Glory Road.* New York: Pocket Books, 1964.
_____, *A Stillness at Appomatox.* New York: Pocket Books, 1953.
Davis, William. *Death in the Trenches.* [Petersburg] Alexandria, Virginia: Time-Life, 1986.
Eaton, Clement. *History of the Southern Confederacy.* New York: Collier, 1961.
Gibbons, Tony. *Warships and Naval Battles of the Civil War.* New York: Gallery Books, 1989.
Korn, Jerry. *Pursuit to Appomatox.* Alexandria, Virginia: Time-Life, 1987.
Leech, Margaret. *Reveille in Washington.* New York: Grosset & Dunlap, 1941.
Lloyd, Mark. *Combat Uniforms of the Civil War.* New York: Mallard Press, 1990.
Monaghan, Jay. *Diplomat in Carpet Slippers.* New York: Bobbs-Merrill, 1945.

BIBLIOGRAPHY (continued)

Articles on some specific subjects

Atlanta Campaign and March through Georgia
"Atlanta Campaign" [whole issue]. *CWTI*, July, 1964.
Luvass, Jay. "Joseph Johnston, a Reappraisal." *CWTI*, January, 1966.

Congress
Koenig, Louis. "The Most Unpopular Man in the North." *AH*, February, 1964.
Long, E.B. "The True Believers: The Committee on the Conduct of the War." *CWTI*, August, 1981.
Rossiter, Clinton. "Our Two Greatest Presidents." *AH*, February, 1959.

Conscription (the draft).
Harrison, Lowell. "Conscription in the Confederacy." *CWTI*, July, 1970.
Murdock, Eugene. "New York's Civil War Bounty Brokers." *JAH*, September, 1966.
Rudolph, Jack. "Taking Up Arms." *CWTI*, April, 1984.

Davis, Jefferson
Satterfield, Paul. "Lincoln and Davis, Their Similarities." *CWT*, May, 1960.
Wiley, Bell. "Jefferson Davis, an Appraisal." *CWTI*, April, 1967.

Entertainment
Bentley, William. "The Great Snowball Fight." *CWTI*, January, 1967.
Gregory, L.H. "An 1862 Baseball Guide." *CWT*, October, 1959.
Mahar, William. "March to the Music." *CWTI*, September, 1984.
Wiley, Bell. "Life in the South." *CWTI*, January, 1970.

Life in the North
Klein, Frederic. "Life in the North." *CWTI*, February, 1970.
Ross, Irwin. "Tom Thumb—27-inch Giant." *AHI*, June, 1968.
Wert, Jeffry. "The Great Civil War Gold Hoax." *CWTI*, April, 1980.

Lincoln, Abraham
Oates, Stephen. "Lincoln: the Man, the Myth." *CWTI*, February, 1984.
Williams, T. Harry. "Lincoln: the Military Strategist." *CWT*, October, 1959.

Peace Movements
Klein, Frederic. "The Great Copperhead Conspiracy." *CWTI*, June, 1965.
Wolf, Adolph. "Shame on Illinois." *CWTI*, December, 1978.

Volunteers
Stutler, Boyd. "Girl Spy for the Confederacy" [Belle Boyd]. *CWT*, April, 1960.
Thomas, Martha. "Amazing Mary" [Walker]. *CWTI*, March, 1984.
Weinert, Richard. "Federal Spies in Richmond." *CWTI*, February, 1965.

Wilderness, Battle of
Cadwallader, Sylvanus. "Three Years with Grant." *AH*, October, 1955.
Cullan, Joseph. "Battle of the Wilderness." *CWTI*, April, 1971.
Melcher, Holman. "We Were Cut Off." *CWTI*, December, 1969.